Uncover 2

Student's Book

Ben Goldstein · Ceri Jones

with Kathryn O'Dell

CAMBRIDGE
UNIVERSITY PRESS

University Printing House, Cambridge CB2 8BS, United Kingdom

One Liberty Plaza, 20th Floor, New York, NY 10006, USA

477 Williamstown Road, Port Melbourne, VIC 3207, Australia

314–321, 3rd Floor, Plot 3, Splendor Forum, Jasola District Centre, New Delhi – 110025, India

79 Anson Road, #06–04/06, Singapore 079906

Cambridge University Press is part of the University of Cambridge.

It furthers the University's mission by disseminating knowledge in the pursuit of education, learning and research at the highest international levels of excellence.

www.cambridge.org
Information on this title: www.cambridge.org/9781107493209

© Cambridge University Press 2015

First published 2015

20 19 18 17 16 15 14 13

Printed in the United Kingdom by CPI Group (UK), Croydon CR0 4YY

A catalog record for this publication is available from the British Library.

ISBN 978-1-107-49320-9 Student's Book 2
ISBN 978-1-107-49323-0 Student's Book with Online Workbook and Online Practice 2
ISBN 978-1-107-49331-5 Teacher's Book 2
ISBN 978-1-107-49328-5 Workbook with Online Practice 2
ISBN 978-1-107-49338-4 Presentation Plus Disc 2
ISBN 978-1-107-49333-9 Class Audio CDs 2
ISBN 978-1-107-49335-3 DVD 2

Additional resources for this publication at www.cambridge.org/uncover

The publishers have no responsibility for the persistence or accuracy
of URLs for external or third-party Internet websites referred to in this publication,
and do not guarantee that any content on such websites is, or will remain,
accurate or appropriate. Information regarding prices, travel timetables and other
factual information given in this work is correct at the time of first printing but
Cambridge University Press does not guarantee the accuracy of such information
thereafter.

Art direction, book design, layout services, and photo research: QBS Learning
Audio production: John Marshall Media

Acknowledgments

Many teachers, coordinators, and educators shared their opinions, their ideas, and their experience to help create *Uncover*. The authors and publisher would like to thank the following people and their schools for their help in shaping the series.

In Mexico:

María Nieves Maldonado Ortiz (Colegio Enrique Rébsamen); Héctor Guzmán Pineda (Liceo Europeo); Alfredo Salas López (Campus Universitario Siglo XXI); Rosalba Millán Martínez (IIPAC [Instituto Torres Quintero A.C.]); Alejandra Rubí Reyes Badillo (ISAS [Instituto San Angel del Sur]); José Enrique Gutiérrez Escalante (Centro Escolar Zama); Gabriela Juárez Hernández (Instituto de Estudios Básicos Amado Nervo); Patricia Morelos Alonso (Instituto Cultural Ingles, S.C.); Martha Patricia Arzate Fernández, (Colegio Valladolid); Teresa González, Eva Marina Sánchez Vega (Colegio Salesiano); María Dolores León Ramírez de Arellano, (Liceo Emperadores Aztecas); Esperanza Medina Cruz (Centro Educativo Francisco Larroyo); Nubia Nelly Martínez García (Salesiano Domingo Savio); Diana Gabriela González Benítez (Colegio Ghandi); Juan Carlos Luna Olmedo (Centro Escolar Zama); Dulce María Pascual Granados (Esc. Juan Palomo Martínez); Roberto González, Fernanda Audirac (Real Life English Center); Rocio Licea (Escuela Fundación Mier y Pesado); Diana Pombo (Great Union Institute); Jacobo Cortés Vázquez (Instituto María P. de Alvarado); Michael John Pryor (Colegio Salesiano Anáhuac Chapalita)

In Brazil:

Renata Condi de Souza (Colégio Rio Branco); Sônia Maria Bernal Leites (Colégio Rio Branco); Élcio Souza (Centro Universitário Anhaguera de São Paulo); Patricia Helena Nero (Private teacher); Célia Elisa Alves de Magalhães (Colégio Cruzeiro-Jacarepaguá); Lilia Beatriz Freitas Gussem (Escola Parque-Gávea); Sandra Maki Kuchiki (Easy Way Idiomas); Lucia Maria Abrão Pereira Lima (Colégio Santa Cruz-São Paulo); Deborah de Castro Ferroz de Lima Pinto (Mundinho Segmento); Clara Vianna Prado (Private teacher); Ligia Maria Fernandes Diniz (Escola Internacional de Alphaville); Penha Aparecida Gaspar Rodrigues (Colégio Salesiano Santa Teresinha); Silvia Castelan (Colégio Santa Catarina de Sena); Marcelo D'Elia (The Kids Club Guarulhos); Malyina Kazue Ono Leal (Colégio Bandeirantes); Nelma de Mattos Santana Alves (Private teacher); Mariana Martins Machado (Britannia Cultural); Lilian Bluvol Vaisman (Curso Oxford); Marcelle Belfort Duarte (Cultura Inglesa-Duque de Caxias); Paulo Dantas (Britannia International English); Anauã Carmo Vilhena (York Language Institute); Michele Amorim Estellita (Lemec – Lassance Modern English Course); Aida Setton (Colégio Uirapuru); Maria Lucia Zaorob (CEL-LEP); Marisa Veiga Lobato (Interlíngua Idiomas); Maria Virgínia Lebrón (Independent consultant); Maria Luiza Carmo (Colégio Guilherme Dumont Villares/CEL-LEP); Lucia Lima (Independent consultant); Malyina Kazue Ono Leal (Colégio Bandeirantes); Debora Schisler (Seven Idiomas); Helena Nagano (Cultura Inglesa); Alessandra de Campos (Alumni); Maria Lúcia Sciamarelli (Colégio Divina Providência); Catarina Kruppa (Cultura Inglesa); Roberto Costa (Freelance teacher/consultant); Patricia McKay Aronis (CEL-LEP); Claudia Beatriz Cavalieri (By the World Idiomas); Sérgio Lima (Vermont English School); Rita Miranda (IBI – [Instituto Batista de Idiomas]); Maria de Fátima Galery (Britain English School); Marlene Almeida (Teacher Trainer Consultant); Flávia Samarane (Colégio Logosófico); Maria Tereza Vianna (Greenwich Schools); Daniele Brauer (Cultura Inglesa/AMS Idiomas); Allessandra Cierno (Colégio Santa Dorotira); Helga Silva Nelken (Greenwich Schools/Colégio Edna Roriz); Regina Marta Bazzoni (Britain English School); Adriano Reis (Greenwich Schools); Vanessa Silva Freire de Andrade (Private teacher); Nilvane Guimarães (Colégio Santo Agostinho)

In Ecuador:

Santiago Proaño (Independent teacher trainer); Tania Abad (UDLA [Universidad de Las Americas]); Rosario Llerena (Colegio Isaac Newton); Paúl Viteri (Colegio Andino); Diego Maldonado (Central University); Verónica Vera (Colegio Tomás Moro); Mónica Sarauz (Colegio San Gabriel); Carolina Flores (Colegio APCH); Boris Cadena, Vinicio Reyes (Colegio Benalcázar); Deigo Ponce (Colegio Gonzaga); Byron Freire (Colegio Nuestra Señora del Rosario)

The authors and publisher would also like to thank the following contributors, script writers, and collaborators for their inspired work in creating *Uncover*:
Anna Whitcher, Janet Gokay, Kathryn O'Dell, Lynne Robertson, and Dana Henricks

1 Traditions

BE CURIOUS

Carpets of Dagestan

What's your favorite place in town?

A Very Indian Wedding

1. Where are the women?

2. What are they like? How are they different from other people in the photo?

3. Do you ever wear traditional clothes? When?

UNIT CONTENTS

Vocabulary Categories; clothes and objects
Grammar Simple present review with *be* and *have*; *whose* and possessives
Listening Whose shoes are they?

Vocabulary: Categories

1. Label the sets of traditional and modern pictures with the correct words.

art   clothing   food   ✓music   places   sports

1. _____ *music*   2. _____

3. _____   4. _____

5. _____   6. _____

2. Listen, check, and repeat.
1.02

3. Do the pictures in Exercise 1 show modern or traditional things? Check (✓) the correct answers.

Photo	a	b	c	d	e	f	g	h	i	j	k	l
Traditional	✓											
Modern		✓										

NOTICE IT
Another word for **clothing** is **clothes. Clothing** is usually used for the general category. **Clothes** is usually used for specific items.
There are two clothing stores in the mall.
I need some new clothes.

Speaking: Likes and dislikes

4. YOUR TURN Work with a partner. Do you like traditional or modern things for the categories in Exercise 1? Can you name any traditional and modern things for each category?

I like modern music. Hip-hop is modern. I don't like traditional music. Jazz is traditional.

I like traditional and modern sports. Sumo wrestling is traditional. Basketball is modern.

Workbook, p. 2

Reading At Home in Two Worlds; Our Summer Tradition; Colorful Hands and Heads
Conversation Keeping a conversation going
Writing A description of a family tradition

OLD and NEW

At Home *in* Two Worlds

Meet Maria! She is 14, and she lives in Otavalo, Ecuador. She has a traditional and a modern life. She lives in a modern house with her family. Maria has a brother. He's 17. She also has a sister. She's 12. Maria and her family make traditional art, and they sell it at a big market in Otavalo. They sell their art online, too. Maria's brother and father are also musicians, and they play traditional music. Maria likes traditional music, but she also listens to modern rock music at home.

Maria doesn't have modern clothes. She wears traditional clothes and jewelry. She eats traditional food with her family. She has meat with corn, potatoes, or beans. After school, she sometimes eats in modern restaurants with her friends. Maria speaks Quechua, an ancient Incan language, with her parents. She speaks Spanish with her brother, sister, and friends. She and her sister also have English classes at school. Maria likes her traditional and modern life!

Reading: An article about life in Otavalo, Ecuador

1. **Look at the photos. Is the family modern or traditional?**

 2. **Read and listen to the article. Who is in Maria's family? What do they do?**

3. **Read the article again. Check (✓) the things that are true for Maria. Sometimes both answers are possible.**

   1. ☐ lives in a traditional house   ☐ lives in a modern house
   2. ☐ has a younger sister   ☐ has an older sister
   3. ☐ has one brother   ☐ has two brothers
   4. ☐ listens to traditional music   ☐ listens to modern music
   5. ☐ wears traditional clothes   ☐ wears modern clothes
   6. ☐ eats traditional food   ☐ eats modern food

4. **YOUR TURN** **Work with a partner. How are you like Maria? How are you different?**

   Maria is 14, and I'm . . .

Grammar: Simple present review with *be* and *have*

5. Complete the chart.

Use the simple present of be to identify people and give locations and dates.
Use the simple present of have to talk about possessions, characteristics, and relationships.

be	have
Wh- questions and answers	
Where **are** you? I'm in Otavalo. I'm _____ in Quito.	When **do** you _____ art class? I **have** art at 10:00. I **don't have** art at 9:00.
How old _____ she? She's 14. She **isn't** 17.	What **does** she **have** for dinner? She _____ meat. She **doesn't have** fish.
Who **are** they? They _____ Maria's parents. They **aren't** her grandparents.	What **do** they **have**? They **have** a computer. They _____ a desk.
Yes/No questions and answers	
_____ you in Otavalo? Yes, I **am**. / No, I'm **not**.	**Do** you **have** art at 10:00? Yes, I _____. / No, I **don't**.
Is she 14? Yes, she _____. / No, she **isn't**.	_____ she **have** meat for dinner? Yes, she **does**. / No, she **doesn't**.
Are they Maria's parents? Yes, they **are**. / No, they _____.	Do they **have** a computer? Yes, they **do**. / No, they _____.

> Check your answers: Grammar reference, p. 106

6. Match the questions with the answers.

1. Is your brother tall? _c_
2. Are they from Ecuador? ___
3. Where are you? ___
4. How many sisters do you have? ___
5. Does Jake have a truck? ___

a. I have three.
b. I'm in my English class.
c. No, he's not.
d. No, he doesn't.
e. Yes, they are.

7. Complete the conversations with the correct form of *be* or *have*.

1. **A:** When _____ your music class?

   B: It _____ on Monday.

2. **A:** _____ Kate and Dennis _____ a truck?

   B: Yes, they _____. They _____ two trucks.

3. **A:** _____ your parents home?

   B: No, they _____. They _____ at work right now.

4. **A:** _____ your house small?

   B: No, it _____. It _____ big.

Speaking: My life

8. **YOUR TURN** Work with a partner. Tell your partner about something modern and something traditional in your life.

> I have a traditional house. It's very old. My clothes are modern. They . . .

BE CURIOUS — Find out about carpet makers in Russia. What is life like in Dagestan? (Workbook, p. 72)

Discovery EDUCATION

1.1 CARPETS OF DAGESTAN

MYThings

Listening: Whose shoes are they?

1. Do your parents or grandparents have things from the past? What do they have?

2. Listen to Wendy and Josh talk about old things in their grandparents' house. Check (✓) the people the things belong to.

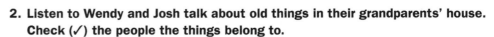

- ☐ father
- ☐ mother
- ☐ grandfather
- ☐ grandmother
- ☐ great-grandfather
- ☐ great-grandmother

3. Listen again. Circle the adjectives that describe the things Wendy and Josh find. There is more than one answer for each item.
   1. First object: **big / small / heavy / colorful / slow**
   2. Second object: **new / old / cool / old-fashioned**
   3. Third object: **white / black / big / small**

Vocabulary: Clothes and objects

4. Match the words with the correct pictures. Then listen and check your answers.

   1. _e_ a computer
   2. ___ a dress
   3. ___ a hat
   4. ___ a jacket
   5. ___ a pen
   6. ___ a photograph / a photo
   7. ___ a telephone / a phone
   8. ___ a television / a TV
   9. ___ a watch
   10. ___ shoes

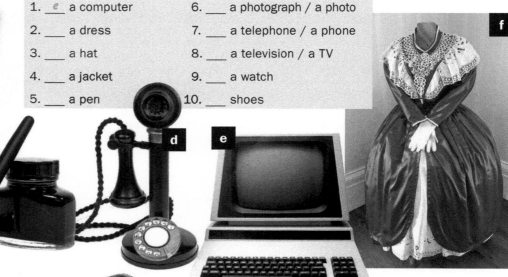

YOUR TURN Work with a partner. What are the items in Exercise 4 like today?

TVs are big today, and they have flat screens. TV shows are in color.

Grammar: *whose* and possessives

6. Complete the chart.

Use whose to ask about possession.
Use a name/noun + 's, a possessive adjective, or a possessive pronoun to show possession.

Whose	_____ computer is it? / **Whose** is it? **Whose** shoes are they? / **Whose** are they?		
Possessive *'s or s'*	It's Dad**'s** computer. They're our grandmother_____ shoes. That's our grandparent**s'** house.		
Possessive adjectives	It's **his** computer. They're **her** shoes. That's **their** house.	my your _____ her its our _____	
Possessive pronouns	It's **his**. They're **hers**. That's **theirs**.	mine yours his _____ its ours _____	

 Check your answers: Grammar reference, p. 106

7. Write questions and answers for the information in the chart. Use possessive *'s* and *s'* for the answers.

	Doug	Sofia	my cousins
1. hat		✓	
2. TV			✓
3. pens	✓		

1. *Whose hat is it? It's Sofia's hat.* _____
2. _____
3. _____

Get it RIGHT!

Do not confuse *whose* with *who's*:
who's = who is.
Whose phone is this?
NOT: ~~**Who's** phone is this?~~

8. Rewrite the sentences two ways. Use possessive adjectives and possessive pronouns.

1. It's my sisters' soccer ball.   *It's their soccer ball. It's theirs.* _____

2. They're Jack's paintings.   _____

3. It's my aunt's jacket.   _____

Speaking: Whose is it?

9. **YOUR TURN** Work with a small group. Each person puts two small items in a bag. The others don't look. Take out an item and have the others guess whose it is. Take turns.

Whose pen is it?

It's Doris' pen.

Say it RIGHT!

If a name ends in -s, add *'s* after the final -s. You can also just use an apostrophe (') after the final -s. Both are correct, and they are pronounced the same way. For example, *Lucas's* and *Lucas'* both sound like *Lucases*. Listen to the sentences.

Lucas has hats. = They're Lucas's hats. / They're Lucas' hats.

Pay attention to the way you pronounce your classmates' names with the possessive in Exercise 9.

Workbook, pp. 4–5

New TRADITIONS

Conversation: A cool tradition

 1. **REAL TALK** Watch or listen to the teenagers. Check (✓) their favorite places.

☐ a bedroom ☐ a gym ☐ a restaurant ☐ an ice cream shop
☐ a computer lab ☐ a library ☐ a stadium ☐ a movie theater
☐ a park ☐ a mall ☐ a supermarket

2. **YOUR TURN** What's *your* favorite place in town? Tell your partner.

 3. Listen to Tom telling Eva about a family tradition. Complete the conversation.

USEFUL LANGUAGE: Keeping a conversation going

| Tell me about it. | That's interesting. | Really? | Then what? |

Eva: Hey, what's that?

Tom: It's my **grandfather's** old **watch**. Well, now it's my **watch**!

Eva: ¹_____

Tom: Yeah. We have this cool tradition for my **grandfather's** birthday.

Eva: ²_____

Tom: Well, we always have a party **in the park**. It's **his** favorite place. We eat traditional food. We have **burgers** and, of course, birthday cake.

Eva: ³_____

Tom: Well, we never give gifts to my **grandfather**. After we eat, **he** gives *us* gifts.

Eva: ⁴_____ Why does he do that?

Tom: He wants us to have his things. So, now I have **his** cool **watch**!

4. Practice the conversation with a partner.

5. **YOUR TURN** Repeat the conversation in Exercise 3, but change the words in purple. Use the information in the chart for one conversation and your own ideas for another.

		My ideas
Person	aunt	
Item	scarf	
Place	in a restaurant	
Food	tacos	

Our Summer Tradition

by Carla Lucero

I have a big Italian family, and we have an unusual tradition. On the last day of school, we always have dinner at an Italian restaurant. We celebrate the start of summer! There are always a lot of people at the restaurant — my parents, my grandparents, my brother, my sister, my cousins, and me!

We have traditional Italian food. There are many great dishes on the menu, like minestrone soup and pasta. We also have dessert. There is traditional Italian music at the restaurant, too. After dinner, we go to my grandparents' house and watch an Italian movie. Then we look at family photos. It's really fun.

Reading to write: A family tradition

6. **Look at the photo. Where are the people? Who do you think they are? Read the article to check.**

> *Focus on* **CONTENT**
> When you write about a tradition, include this information:
> - what   - why
> - when   - who
> - where

7. **Read Carla's article again. Find examples for the categories in the Focus on Content box.**

> *Focus on* **LANGUAGE**
> **there is / there are**
> Use **there is / there are** to give information about what, when, where, why, and who in a description of something, such as a family tradition.
> - **There is** *a big table in the restaurant.*
> - **There are** *many musicians at our summer picnic.*

8. **Find examples of *There is / There are* in Carla's article.**

9. **Complete the sentence with *There is* or *There are*.**

   1. _____ a lot of modern art at the museum.
   2. _____ three birthdays in my family in June.
   3. _____ many books in our house.
   4. _____ a singer in the restaurant.
   5. _____ a lot of people at the wedding.
   6. _____ a good show on TV.

Writing: My family tradition

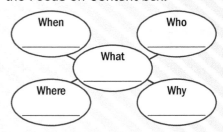

◯ **PLAN**
Choose a tradition in your family. Make a word web with the topics from the Focus on Content box.

When   Who
What
Where   Why

◯ **WRITE**
Now write about the tradition. Use your notes to help you. Write at least 60 words.

◯ **CHECK**
Check your writing. Can you answer "yes" to these questions?

- Is information for each category from the Focus on Content box in your article?

- Do you use *there is* and *there are* correctly?

COLORFUL HANDS AND HEADS

What color is your hair? In many cultures, people change their hair color for some traditions. Face and body painting is a tradition in many places, too. These traditions are new and old!

The Romanian soccer team at the World Cup

Citrus College fans at a soccer game

_____

Some sports teams color their hair with their team colors. For example, a high school swim team has blue hair for a swimming event. A professional soccer team has yellow hair for the World Cup. Sports fans often paint their faces with school colors, too. At many sports events, there are people in school colors from head to toe!

A wedding in, India

_____

In some traditional weddings in India, the bride has designs on her hands with henna, a special paint. During the wedding, the groom colors the middle of the bride's hair red. It is a symbol of marriage.

A teenager in the Omo Valley

_____

It is hot and sunny in the Omo Valley in Africa. Mursi and Surma people paint their faces, heads, and bodies with clay from the earth. It protects them from the sun. It is a tradition, and it is also art. They have white, yellow, red, and gray designs on their faces and bodies. They have colorful clay in their hair, too, and sometimes they make and wear interesting hats.

New or old, hair coloring and face painting are interesting traditions!

Culture: Hair coloring and face painting traditions

1. **Look at the photos. Where are the people? What colors do you see?**

2. **Read the article. Complete the text with the headings. Then listen and check your answers.**

   Tradition and Art   A New Sports Tradition
   An Old Wedding Tradition

3. **Read the article again. Are the sentences true (T) or false (F)?**

   1. A bride in India has paint on her hands. ___

   2. A bride in India has blue paint in her hair. ___

   3. It is cold in the Omo Valley. ___

   4. Sports players never have colored hair. ___

4. **YOUR TURN Work with a partner. Ask and answer the question.**

   What are some sports and wedding traditions from your culture?

Vocabulary

1. Label the photos with the correct categories.

art	food	places
clothing	music	sports

1. _Music_   2. _Food_

3. _Sports_   4. _clothing_

5. _Places_   6. _ART_

2. Complete the sentences with the correct words.

computer	hat	photo	TV
jacket	phone	shoes	watch

1. I have a _Hat_ on my head.

2. I use my _computer_ to do my homework.

3. There are a lot of good shows on _Watch_.

4. Lori is on the _____. Do you want to talk to her?

5. It's cold! I have on a _Jacket_ over my shirt.

6. See this _photo_ of my mother? It's from 1980!

7. Sam and Ann left their _Shoes_ by the door.

8. I don't have a _TV_, so I check the time on my phone.

Grammar

3. Circle the correct words.

Vicky: Hey, Paolo! ¹**Is / Are / Do / Does** you have an art class this year?

Paolo: Yes, I ²**am / am not / do / don't**. I ³**am / is / has / have** two art classes.

Vicky: ⁴**Is / Are / Do / Does** Mrs. Meyers one of your teachers?

Paolo: No, she ⁵**is / isn't / does / doesn't**. Why?

Vicky: Oh, she ⁶**is / isn't / does / doesn't** my aunt. She ⁷**is / are / has / have** three art classes this year.

Paolo: I see. My art teachers ⁸**is / are / has / have** Mr. Klein and Ms. Rodriguez.

4. Match the sentences with the same meaning.

1. It's my volleyball. _a_   a. It's mine.

2. It's Sandra's dress. _d_   b. It's yours.

3. It's Ted's pen. _c_   c. It's his.

4. It's your sandwich. _b_   d. It's hers.

Useful language

5. Circle the correct answers.

1. **A:** We have an unusual tradition in my family.
   B: Tell me _____ it.
   a. on   b. in   **c. about**

2. **A:** We always have a big dinner for my birthday.
   B: _____? Me, too.
   a. When   **b. Really**   c. Then

3. **A:** Why is your face green?
   B: Oh, it's for the soccer game.
   A: That's _____. Is green your school color?
   a. always   b. never   **c. interesting**

4. **A:** We always have a picnic at the park on Saturdays.
   B: Then _____?
   a. what   b. why   **c. where**
   A: We usually play games.

PROGRESS CHECK: Now I can . . .

☐ identify and talk about modern and traditional things.	☐ keep a conversation going.
☐ talk about modern and traditional things in my life.	☐ write about a family tradition.
☐ ask and answer questions about possessions.	☐ talk about sports, weddings, and other traditions.

2 WHAT'S Playing?

A Life on Broadway

What types of TV shows do you like watching?

Mumbai: From Computers to Film

Who's Real?

1. What are the people watching?

2. How do you think they feel about it?

3. Do you like to do this activity?

UNIT CONTENTS
Vocabulary Types of movies; types of TV shows
Grammar Simple present review; adverbs of frequency; verb + infinitive or -ing form (gerund)
Listening Deciding what to watch

Vocabulary: Types of movies

1. Match the phrases (a–i) with the correct movie posters.

√ a. an action movie   ✓ d. a drama   √ g. a martial arts movie

√ b. an animated movie   √ e. a fantasy movie   √ h. a musical

√ c. a comedy   √ f. a horror movie   √ i. a romance movie

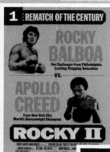

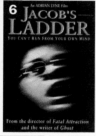

1. _d_
2. _e_
3. _h_
4. _b_
5. _g_
6. _f_
7. _i_
8. _c_
9. _a_

2. Listen, check, and repeat.

3. Write the types of movies.

1. A lot of things happen quickly in this type of movie.   _action movie_

2. The music in this type of film is great, and the actors are very good singers.   _Musical_

3. People say these movies are for children, but adults watch them, too.   _Fantasy_

4. This type of movie usually has events that couldn't happen in real life and great special effects.   _Action Movie_

5. The story and characters in these movies are very funny. They make you laugh!   _Comedy_ _Animated_

Speaking: More movies

4. **YOUR TURN** Work with a partner. Name a movie for each type of movie.

> *Bend It Like Beckham* is a drama.

> *Twilight* is a drama, too. And it's also a romance movie.

5. What are some of your favorite movies? What types of movies are they?

> One of my favorite movies is *The Hunger Games*. It's a fantasy and an action movie. I also like . . .

 Say it RIGHT!

The letters *sh*, *ci*, and *ti* can make the /ʃ/ sound. Listen to the sentence.

She liked the spe**ci**al effects in the ac**ti**on movie.

Listen to the words in Exercise 1 again. Which other word makes the /ʃ/ sound? What letters make the sound?

 Workbook, p. 8

Reading Cinema's Best Villains; My All-Time Favorite Movie; Hooray for Bollywood!
Conversation Asking for and giving opinions
Writing A movie review

Let's Go *to the* Movies!

Welcome to my blog about movies.

I sometimes go to the movies three times a week! How often do you go to the movies?

My favorite types of films are horror, action, and fantasy movies. What types of movies do you like?

I also love the "bad guys" in movies. Here are my top three villains.

Cinema's Best Villains
by Erica Thompson

Cruella De Vil
Movie: *101 Dalmatians* Actor: Betty Lou Gerson (voice) Famous phrase: "You beasts!" I don't like this movie very much, but Cruella is a great villain. She loves puppies and especially Dalmatians – because she wants to wear them!

Darth Vader
Movie: *Star Wars V: The Empire Strikes Back* Actor: David Prowse Famous phrase: "You don't know the power of the dark side!" This is my favorite movie, and Darth Vader is the perfect villain because he never shows his face. He also speaks with a strange voice.

The Penguin
Movie: *Batman Returns* Actor: Danny DeVito Famous phrase: "Nyuk, nyuk, nyuk." The Penguin is a villain in some of the Batman movies, TV shows, and comic books. His real name is Oswold Cobblepot. Sometimes he's funny, and sometimes he's scary, but he's always dangerous. I like him best in *Batman Returns*.

Who is your favorite movie villain?

Reading: A blog about movie villains

1. Look at the photos of the three movie characters. What types of movies do you think they are from?

2. Read and listen to the blog post. Which of the movies that Erica writes about does she like?

DID YOU KNOW...?
David Prowse was Darth Vader, but he didn't talk in the movie. Another actor, James Earl Jones, was Darth Vader's voice.

3. Read the blog post again. Answer the questions.

   1. What types of movies does Erica like?
   Action, Horror and fantasy

   2. Why does Cruella De Vil like puppies?
   Yes, she like's

   3. Why does Erica think Darth Vader is a perfect villain?
   Yes, she think's

   4. What is the Penguin's real name?
   Is oswold cobblepot

   5. Which movie doesn't Erica like? Which one is her favorite?
   lol dalmatons and ERIKa Favorite is Starcubes V

4. **YOUR TURN** Work with a partner. Do you agree with Erica's best villains? Who are your top three favorite movie villains? Why?

> One of my favorite villains is . . . because . . .

Grammar: Simple present review

5. Complete the chart.

Use the simple present to talk about routines, habits, and facts.

Wh- questions	Affirmative answers	Negative answers
What movies __do__ you __like__?	I **like** horror movies.	I **don't like** musicals.
How often **does** Erica **go** to the movies?	She __likes__ to the movies three times a week.	She __likes__ to the movies on Sundays.
Yes/No questions	Short answers	
Do you **like** horror movies?	Yes, I __do__.	No, I **don't**.
__Does__ Erica __likes__ to the movies?	Yes, she **does**.	No, she __doen't__.
Contractions do not = __don't__		does not = __doen't__

> Check your answers: Grammar reference, p. 107

6. Circle the correct words. Then answer the questions with information about you.

1. (Do) / Does you (go) / goes to the movies on the weekends?
   What types of movies (do) / does you (see) / sees?
   Yes, I do. I see action movies and comedies.

2. (What) / Where types of movies (do) / does your friends (like) / likes?
   (Do) / Does you (like) / likes the same types of movies?
   _____

3. **How** / (When) late (do) / **does** the movie theaters (stay) / **stays** open in your city?
   _____

Spell it **RIGHT!**

I/you/we/they	he/she/it
go	go**es**
study	stud**ies**
teach	teach**es**

7. Rewrite the sentences. Put the adverbs of frequency in the correct places.

1. Jamie watches movies with his friends. (usually)
   Jamie usually watches movies with his friends.

2. Amy buys popcorn at the movies. (always)
   Amy always buys popcorn at the movie.

3. Carol reads movie reviews online. (sometimes)
   Carol sometimes reads movies reviews online.

4. I'm at the movie theater early. (often)
   Often I'm at the movie theater early

Speaking: Movie-watching habits

8. YOUR TURN Work with a partner. Ask and answer questions about where and how often you watch movies.

> Where do you watch movies?

> I usually watch movies at the movie theater.

> I never watch movies at home.

Adverbs of frequency

always   usually   often   sometimes   never

Adverbs of frequency usually come after the verb *be*, but before other verbs.
I'm **never** late. They **never** learn.
Usually and *sometimes* may come before the subject.
Sam **usually** goes to the movies three times a week.
Usually, Sam goes to the movies three times a week.

BE CURIOUS   Find out about a musical on Broadway. Who is involved in *Annie*? (Workbook, p. 74)

●Discovery
EDUCATION

2.1 A LIFE ON BROADWAY

> Workbook, p. 9

WHAT'S ON?

Listening: Deciding what to watch

1. Who do you watch TV with? What shows do you watch together?

 2. Listen to Joanna and Alex decide what to watch on TV. What shows do they want to watch? Write *J* (Joanna), *A* (Alex), or *B* (both).

1. *Big Brother* __A__   2. *Elementary* __B__   3. *The Big Bang Theory* __J__

 3. Listen again. Are the statements true (*T*) or false (*F*)?

1. Sheldon and Leonard are scientists on a TV show. __T__ ✓

2. Penny is Joanna's neighbor. __F__ ✓

3. Alex saw *Big Brother* in the past. __T__ ✓

4. Joanna likes animated shows. __F__ ✓

5. Alex and Joanna both like dramas. __T__ ✓

Vocabulary: Types of TV shows

 4. Label the pictures with the correct words. Then listen and check your answers.

a cartoon	a game show	a soap opera
a crime series	a reality TV show	a talk show
✓ a documentary	a sitcom	the news

1. ___*a documentary*___   2. ___a crime series___   3. ___soap opera___

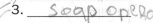

4. ___cartoon___   5. ___sitcom___   6. ___a talk shows___

7. ___The news___   8. ___game show___   9. ___a really tv___

5. **YOUR TURN** Work with a partner. Talk about how often you watch each type of TV show.

> I never watch documentaries. I often watch crime series.

Grammar: Verb + infinitive or -*ing* form (gerund)

6. Complete the chart.

Verb + infinitive	Verb + -*ing* form (gerund)
They **want to watch** a drama.	Sheldon **dislikes try**_ing_ new things.
He **needs** _to_ **see** who gets voted off *Big Brother*.	Leonard **enjoys trying** different things.

Verb + infinitive or -*ing* form (gerund)
I **like to read** comic books. I **like reading** comic books.
They **love to read** comic books. They **love** _to_ comic books.
She **hates to watch** reality TV shows. She **hates watching** reality TV shows.
He **prefers** _to get_ the news online. He **prefers getting** the news online.

> Check your answers: Grammar reference, p. 107

7. Complete the questions and answers with the -*ing* form (gerund) or infinitive of the verbs. Sometimes more than one answer is possible.

1. **A:** Do you want _____to get_____ (get) this big screen TV?

   B: No. I hate _to pay_ (pay) full price. Let's see if one is on sale. ✓

2. **A:** I like _to watch_ (watch) movies online. ✓

   B: Not me. I prefer _going_ (go) to a movie theater. ✓

3. **A:** Ugh! I need _to wash_ (wash) the dishes before we watch TV. ✓

   B: Do you dislike _doing_ (do) them? I can help you. ✓

4. **A:** Does your sister like _to work_ (work) for a TV studio? ✓

   B: Yes. She loves _to think_ (think) of new ideas for TV shows. ✓

8. **YOUR TURN** **Use the words and your own ideas to write sentences that are true for you.**

1. my parents / like / watch / . . . _My parents like watching talk shows._

2. my friends / enjoy / read / . . . _My FRiends enjoy reading manga_

3. I / need / get / . . . _I need geting a shower._

4. I / want / see / . . . _I want seeing this paper._

Get it **RIGHT!**

Use the infinitive or -*ing* form (gerund) of a verb, not the base form, after some verbs.
I **want to write** a TV show. NOT: I **want write** a TV show.
She **loves to watch** TV at night.
OR She **loves watching** TV at night.
NOT She **loves** watch TV at night.

Speaking: TV-watching habits

9. **YOUR TURN** **Read the sentences and check (✓) "Yes" or "No" in the "You" column.**

	You		Your partner	
	Yes	No	Yes	No
I love watching sitcoms.				
I hate to watch documentaries.				
I want to watch less TV.				
I enjoy watching TV shows online.				

10. Work with a partner. Ask and answer questions about the information in Exercise 9. Check (✓) "Yes" or "No" in the "Your partner" column.

Do you like watching sitcoms?

No, I don't. I hate to watch sitcoms.

TV and Movie FAVORITES

Conversation: It's really funny!

1. **REAL TALK** Watch or listen to the teenagers. Check the shows they mention.

☐ animated movies	☐ documentaries	☐ horror movies	☐ soap operas
☐ cartoons	☐ dramas	☐ musicals	☐ sports news
☐ comedies	☐ game shows	☐ reality TV shows	☐ talk shows

2. **YOUR TURN** What types of TV shows do *you* like watching? Tell your partner.

3. Listen to Jay and Tina talking about TV shows. Complete the conversation.

USEFUL LANGUAGE: Asking for and giving opinions

How do you feel about	What do you think about	I think	In my opinion

Jay: Do you watch a lot of TV, Tina?

Tina: Yes, I do.

Jay: What do you like to watch?

Tina: I really like **sitcoms**.

Jay: ¹_____ *Modern Family*?

Tina: That's my favorite show! It's really **funny**!

Jay: I like it, too. ²_____ **reality TV shows**?

Tina: ³_____ they're **boring**. I never watch them. What about you?

Jay: They're OK. I sometimes watch them, but I prefer **game shows**.

Tina: Really? Why?

Jay: ⁴_____, they're **exciting**.

Tina: Yeah, I guess so.

4. Practice the conversation with a partner.

5. **YOUR TURN** Work with a partner. Practice the conversation in Exercise 3 again, but change the words in purple. Use the information in the chart for one conversation and your own ideas for another.

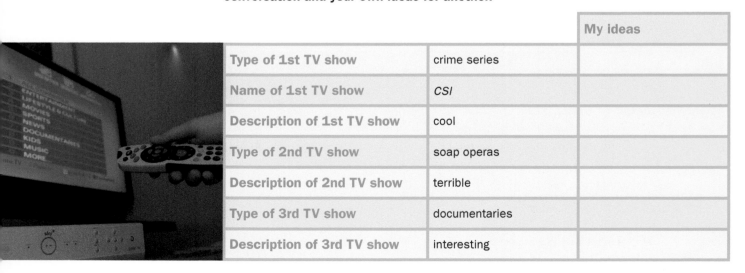

		My ideas
Type of 1st TV show	crime series	
Name of 1st TV show	*CSI*	
Description of 1st TV show	cool	
Type of 2nd TV show	soap operas	
Description of 2nd TV show	terrible	
Type of 3rd TV show	documentaries	
Description of 3rd TV show	interesting	

My All-Time Favorite Movie by Sofia Ramos

My favorite movie is *Twilight*, the first film in the Twilight Saga series. It stars Kristen Stewart as Bella and Robert Pattinson as Edward. The director is Catherine Hardwicke.

The movie is about Bella, a teenage girl in modern times. She moves to Forks, a small town in Washington. She meets Edward, a smart and good-looking classmate. She discovers he is a vampire, but she falls in love with him anyway. Another vampire wants to hurt Bella, so Edward tries to protect her.

I like this movie because the acting is really good. The music and camerawork make it dark and mysterious. I love watching fantasy movies, and this movie combines fantasy and romance.

Reading to write: A movie review

6. Look at the photo in Sofia's movie review. What type of movie do you think it is? Read the review to check.

 Focus on **CONTENT**

When you write a movie review, include this information:
- the main characters and actors
- the time and place
- the director
- the type of movie
- a short description of the story
- why you like it or don't like it

7. Read Sofia's review again. What information from the Focus on Content box does she include in each paragraph?

 Focus on **LANGUAGE**

Connectors *so* and *because*
Use **so** when one event is the result of another event:
- *Edward is smart and good-looking, **so** Bella falls in love with him.*
Use **because** to explain the reason something happens.
- *I like action movies **because** they are exciting.*

8. Find an example of *so* and an example of *because* in Sofia's review.

9. Complete the sentences with *so* or *because.*

1. Harry Potter has special powers, _____ he goes to the Hogwarts School for wizards.
2. Peter Parker becomes Spider-Man _____ a spider bites him.
3. In *Toy Story*, Woody and Buzz get lost, _____ they try to find their way home.
4. At the beginning of *The Lion King*, Simba is sad _____ his father dies.

 Writing: Your movie review

○ **PLAN**
Choose your favorite movie or a movie you saw recently. Include the information in the Focus on Content box and take notes in a chart like the one below.

The main characters and actors	
The director	
The type of movie	
The time and place	
A short description of the story	
Why you like it or don't like it	

○ **WRITE**
Now, write your movie review. Use your notes to help you. Write at least 60 words.

○ **CHECK**
Check your writing. Can you answer "yes" to these questions?
- Is information from the Focus on Content box in your review?
- Do you use *so* and *because* to show how events connect?

Workbook, pp. 12–13

HOORAY for BOLLYWOOD!

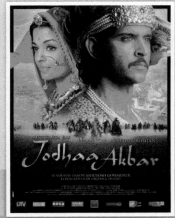

Forget Hollywood! Bollywood is number one in the world of cinema! Bollywood is the name of the Hindi film industry in India. Its home is in Mumbai. Mumbai's name was Bombay in the past, so Bollywood gets its name from *Bombay* and *Hollywood*. Bollywood makes about 1,000 movies every year. That's about two times more than Hollywood. More people watch Bollywood movies, too – over three billion people watch them! About 14 million Indians go to the movies every day.

Bollywood movies are different from Hollywood movies. They are very long and usually last about three or four hours. Many of them are musicals. The movie *Indra Sabha* has the record for the most songs. It has 71 songs in it.

Music and dancing are very important in Bollywood movies. They often contain typical Indian music and traditional Indian dance styles, like Kathak and Bharata Natyam. The dancing helps tell the story in the movie. Bollywood movies also contain modern dance forms, like hip-hop and jazz. The films often include romance, comedy, action, and adventure in their stories.

These movies aren't only popular in India. People around the world love watching them! The movies are usually in Hindi, but there are often subtitles in other languages, like Bengali, Arabic, and English.

Culture: Bollywood movies

1. **Look at the photos. What types of movies do think they are?**

2.08

2. **Read and listen to the article. Check the best description of Bollywood movies.**

   ☐ Traditional Indian movies in several languages

   ☐ Hindi movies, often with singing and dancing

   ☐ Hollywood movies made into Indian movies

3. **Read the article again. Are the sentences *T* (true) or *F* (false)? Correct the false sentences.**

   1. Bollywood is a combination of the words *Bengali* and *Hollywood*. ___

   2. More people go to see Bollywood movies than Hollywood movies. ___

   3. A lot of Bollywood movies are musicals. ___

   4. *Indra Sabha* has the record for the longest movie. ___

   5. Kathak is a type of traditional Indian music. ___

   6. Bollywood movies are popular in many countries. ___

4. **YOUR TURN Work with a partner. Ask and answer the questions.**

   1. Do you want to see a Bollywood movie? Why or why not?

   2. Do you watch Hollywood movies? How often?

   3. Do you prefer to watch Hollywood movies or movies from other countries? What is better about the movies you prefer?

DID YOU KNOW...?
There is often an intermission during Bollywood movies because they are so long. Moviegoers take a short break and often buy snacks during the intermission.

BE CURIOUS
Find out about the city of Mumbai. What is it like? (Workbook, p. 75)

Discovery EDUCATION
2.3 MUMBAI: FROM COMPUTERS TO FILM

UNIT 2 REVIEW

Vocabulary

1. Put the letters in the correct order to make words for different types of movies.

1. aonercm ___Romance___ ✓   4/4
2. meydoc ___Comedy___ ✓
3. nafstya ___Fantasy___ ✓
4. roorhr ___Horror___ ✓

2. Match the types of TV shows to their descriptions.

1. a talk show _b_ ✗ c   3/5
2. a game show _e_ ✓
3. the news _d_ ✓
4. a soap opera _c_ ✗ b
5. a crime series _a_ ✓

a	Police officer Jules Kiln finds new clues to an old mystery on *The Scene*.
b	Today on *Green Street*, Sam is unhappy with Gina. Tara tells Mick her secret.
c	Tom Buckley speaks to the children of famous musicians on *Tell Me Today*.
d	Sarah Carver gives today's top events and weather at 8:00 p.m.
e	Watch three people try to win $25,000 on *Make It Big*.

Grammar

3. Complete the sentences with the simple present forms of the verbs.

do	not like	watch	go

3/4

1. We usually ___watch___ TV in the evening. ✓ Our favorite shows are sitcoms.
2. Casey always ___goes___ to the movies on ✗ the weekends.
3. When ___do___ you usually ___do___ ✓ your homework?
4. Vicky ___not like___ soap operas. She thinks ✗ they're boring.

4. Circle the correct answers. Sometimes both answers are correct.

1. Greg loves **to watch** / (**watching**) sitcoms ✓ at night.
2. Sandra and Kelly want **to see** / (**seeing**) that ✗ new animated movie.
3. I need (**to leave**) / **leaving** the theater right ✓ after the movie.
4. Liv dislikes **to have** / (**having**) the TV on when ✓ she does her homework.

Useful language

5. Circle the correct answers.

Jan: Hey, Doug. How do you ¹(**think**) / **feel** / ✗ **tell** about reality TV shows?

Doug: In my ²**thought** / (**opinion**) / **decision**, ✓ they're terrible.

Jan: Really? I like them.

Doug: Not me. I ³**agree** / (**dislike**) / (**think**) ✓ they're boring.

Jan: Well, I'm going to be on a reality TV show! How do you ⁴(**think**) / **feel** / **tell** ✗ about that?

Doug: Oh, uh, well . . . that's cool, I guess.

3/4

2/4

PROGRESS CHECK: Now I can . . .

- ☐ identify different types of movies.
- ☐ talk about my movie-watching habits.
- ☐ talk about different types of TV shows, preferences, and TV habits.
- ☐ ask for and give opinions.
- ☐ write a movie review.
- ☐ compare Hollywood movies with other movies.

▶ REVIEW UNITS 1–2, Workbook, pp. 14–15

CLIL PROJECT

2.4 Who's Real?, p. 116

3 Spending Habits

Discovery
EDUCATION

BE CURIOUS

Unusual Fun

How do you spend
your money?

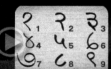
Zero: Past and
Present

1. What do you think the people have in their bags?

2. Do you like to shop alone or with friends? Why?

3. How often do you go shopping? What do you usually buy?

UNIT CONTENTS

Vocabulary	Places to shop; money verbs
Grammar	Present continuous review; simple present vs. present continuous; quantifiers
Listening	Shopping habits

Vocabulary: Places to shop

1. Complete the key in the map with the correct numbers.

7 bank and ATM ✓
10 bookstore ✓
4 clothing store √
6 department store ✓
2 electronics store ✓
1 food court ✓
3 jewelry store ✓
8 music store ✓
11 pharmacy ✓
9 shoe store ✓
5 sporting goods store √

2. Listen, check, and repeat. 🔊 3.01

3. What things are there in each place in Exercise 1?

> There are jeans, T-shirts, and jackets in a clothing store.

> A clothing store also has hats, dresses, and . . .

Speaking: Your favorite stores

4. **YOUR TURN** **Work with a partner. What are your three favorite stores? Why?**

> One of my favorite stores is a department store. There are many different things for sale there. Another favorite store is . . .

5. Now work with the class. Make a list of everyone's favorite stores. Which stores are the top three favorites?

Workbook, p. 16

NOTICE IT
ATM stands for *automated teller machine*. A *teller* is a person in a bank whose job is to receive money from or give money to customers.

🔊 3.02 **Say it RIGHT!**

In one-word compound nouns, the first syllable is stressed. In compound nouns with two or more words, the first syllable of the first word is usually stressed. Listen and repeat the words.

bookstore   **jew**elry store   **spor**ting goods store

Listen and circle the stressed syllable in each compound noun.
food court   music store
clothing store   shoe store

Reading A Day at the Mall in Dubai; Product Reviews; Adopt an Animal
Conversation Making requests when shopping
Writing A product review

STORES *and* MORE

A Day at the Mall in DUBAI

I'm Lucas. I'm from Mexico, but I live in Dubai now because my parents work here. I'm writing about my life in my new city.

Today, I'm at the Dubai Mall with my family. It has about 1,200 stores, including five department stores, two music stores, more than 25 electronics stores, and about 50 shoe stores!

Are we shopping? No, we're not! There are a lot of other things to do at this mall. My dad and my sister are watching the fish in the Aquarium and Underwater Zoo right now. There are more than 33,000 fish – even sharks! My mom and I are skating on the Olympic-size Dubai Ice Rink. It's hot in Dubai, but it's cold at the ice rink! Later, I want to go to the mall's theme park, the Sega Republic. It has 170 games and many rides.

Outside of the mall is the Dancing Fountain. The water goes up 150 meters! At night, the water changes color because the fountain has lights with 25 different colors.

I hope we stay here all day and night!

Reading: An article about a mall in Dubai

1. Look at the photos. What do you see?

3.03

2. Read and listen to the article. Match the photos (a–d) with the places (1–4).

   1. The Aquarium and Underwater Zoo ___

   2. The Dubai Ice Rink ___

   3. Stores in the mall ___

   4. The Dancing Fountain ___

3. Read the article again. Complete the sentences with the correct numbers.

   1. The mall has about _____ stores.

   2. There are about _____ shoe stores in the mall.

   3. The aquarium has over _____ fish.

   4. There are _____ games at the theme park.

   5. The water in the fountain goes up _____ meters.

   6. There are _____ different colors in the fountain lights.

4. **YOUR TURN** Work with a partner. What would you do at the Dubai Mall? Why?

   > I'd go to the ice rink. I like to ice-skate!

DID YOU KNOW...?

The Dubai Mall is one of the biggest malls in the world. More than 50 million people visit it every year.

Grammar: Present continuous review; simple present vs. present continuous

5. Complete the chart.

> Use the present continuous to talk about activities that are happening now.

Wh- questions	Affirmative answers	Negative answers
What **are** you **doing**?	I ___am___ **writing** a book.	I'm **not writing** about my job.
What **is** he __doing__?	He's **skating**.	He's ___not___ **running**.
What ___are___ they **doing**?	They're **watch**ing TV.	They ___aren't___ **skating**.

Yes/No questions		Short answers
___Are___ you **writing** about Dubai?	Yes, I ___am___.	No, I'm ___not___.
___Is___ he **skating**?	Yes, he ___is___.	No, he **isn't**.
Are we **shopping**?	Yes, we **are**.	No, we ___are not___.

> *Remember: Use the simple present for facts, habits, and routines.*
> At night, the water **changes** color. = routine
> Look! The water **is changing** color. = activity happening now

> Check your answers: Grammar reference, p. 108

6. Complete the sentences with the present continuous forms of the verbs.

1. Cassandra ___writing___ (write) a blog about her life in the city.
2. What ___are___ you ___buying___ (buy) at the electronics store?
3. I ___am waiting___ (wait) in line at the pharmacy.
4. We ___aren't shopping___ (not shop) at the mall today.
5. Marta ___I getting / aren't___ (not get) money at the ATM now.

4,5/5

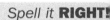

Spell it RIGHT!

The **-ing** form:
For verbs ending in **-e**, remove the **e**, and then add **-ing**: write → writing.
For verbs ending with one vowel and one consonant, double the final consonant: shop → shopping.

7. Complete the conversation with the simple present or the present continuous forms of the verbs.

Abe: Hi, Lori. What ¹___are___ you ___doing___ (do)?

Lori: I ²_____ (shop) with my parents. We ³_____ (look) for a new school bag and clothes at a department store.

Abe: Just in time! School starts on Monday.

Lori: I know. We ⁴_____ (do) the same thing every year. We always ⁵_____ (shop) the weekend before school starts.

Abe: I ⁶_____ (not do) that! I ⁷_____ (buy) my things for school online during the summer.

Lori: That's a good idea! So, what ⁸_____ you _____ (do) right now?

Abe: I ⁹_____ (watch) a movie on TV.

Lori: Lucky you!

Speaking: At the mall

8. YOUR TURN Work with a partner. You are at a mall in different stores. Think of at least five questions you can ask each other on the phone. Use the simple present and present continuous.

> Where are you? What are you doing? Why . . . ?

9. Create a conversation with your partner.

> Where are you? What are you doing?

> I'm in the shoe store. I'm looking for new sneakers. I want ...

BE CURIOUS Find out about places in Dubai. What are some things people do in Dubai? (Workbook, p. 76)

Discovery EDUCATION

3.1 UNUSUAL FUN

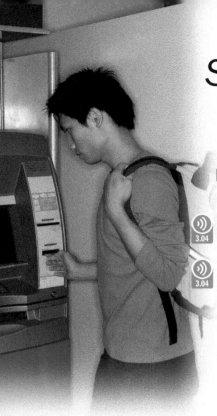

Spending and
SAVING

Listening: Shopping habits

1. **Do you usually shop at stores or online? Why?**

2. **Listen to a reporter talk to teens about shopping and money. What do Josh and Megan have in their shopping bags?**

3. **Listen again. Circle the correct answers.**

   1. Josh wants (a new video game) / a T-shirt. ✓
   2. Josh usually buys clothes at a mall / (online). ✓
   3. It's Megan's / (Josh's) birthday. ✓
   4. Megan has a necklace / (soccer ball) for herself. ✓
   5. Megan wants a new job / (phone). ✓

   5/5

Vocabulary: Money verbs

4. **Look at the pictures. Complete the sentences with the simple present forms of the verbs. Then listen and check your answers.**

✓ borrow	earn	save	withdraw
deposit	lend	spend	

Jordan's friend is selling a bike. It costs $200. Jordan wants to buy the bike, but he only has $50. He ¹ _____borrows_____ money from his aunt. His aunt ² _____lend_____ him $50. He ³ _____save_____ the money in his bank account. He gets a part-time job at a pizza place in the food court, and he ⁴ _____earn_____ $100 a week. He ⁵ _____withdraw_____ some of that money on movies and video games. He ⁶ _____deposit_____ $25 a week for a month and puts it in the bank. Finally, he ⁷ _____spend_____ $200 from the bank, and he buys his friend's bike!

5. **YOUR TURN Work with a partner. Ask and answer the questions.**

   1. Do you earn money? How do you earn it?
   2. Do you usually save money or spend money? What do you spend money on?
   3. Do you ever borrow money? Who lends you money?
   4. Do you ever lend money? Who borrows money from you?
   5. Where do you or your parents deposit and withdraw money?

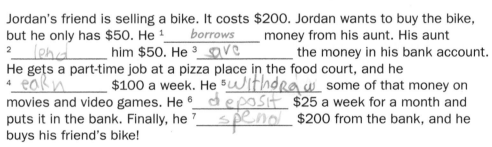

Grammar: Quantifiers

6. Complete the chart.

Use quantifiers to show the amount of something.	
With countable plural nouns	**With uncountable nouns**
How **many** T-shirts do you have?	How **much** money do you have?
I have **some** / _many_ / **enough** T-shirts.	I have _some_ / **a lot of** / **enough** money.
I don't have **many** / _any_ / **a lot of** / **enough** T-shirts.	I **don't** have **much** / **any** / **a lot of** / _enough_ money.
Are there **many** / **any** / _a lot of_ / **enough** T-shirts in your dresser?	Is there _much_ / **any** / **a lot of** / **enough** money in your bank account?
Yes, there are. / No, there aren't.	Yes, there is. / No, there isn't.

Check your answers: Grammar reference, p. 108

> **Get it RIGHT!**
>
> **enough** = as many as needed
> **not enough** = less than what is needed
> **Enough** goes before nouns and after adjectives:
> *I don't have **enough money** to buy a phone.*
> *I'm not **old enough** to get a job.*

7. Circle the correct words.

1. Cynthia has **much** / (**a lot of**) money.

2. I save (**some**) / **any** money every month.

3. Are there **much** / (**any**) department stores in that mall?

4. How (**much**) / **many** time do you spend at the mall?

5. I'm not old **some** / (**enough**) to drive a car.

6. There aren't (**a lot of**) / **much** cars for sale here.

G/6

8. Complete the conversation with the correct words.

a lot of	enough	how much	✓ any	some

Eddie: Oh, no! The bus is coming, and I don't have ¹ _any_ money. Can I borrow ² _some_ money from you?

Maya: Well, I don't have ³ ~~a lot of~~ money. I only have $5. ⁴ _How much_ is a ticket?

Eddie: It's $2.50.

Maya: Oh, OK. I have ⁵ ~~enough~~ money, so I can lend you $2.50. No problem.

Eddie: Thanks!

S15

enough = a lot of

a lot of = enough

Speaking: A money quiz

9. **YOUR TURN** Read the questions and use the words to write answers that are true for you. Then add one more question to the list. Write the answers.

a lot of	some	enough	not enough	not any

1. How much money do you save a month? _____

2. How many times do you go shopping each month? _____

3. How much do you spend on clothes each month? _____

4. _____ _____

10. Work with a partner. Ask and answer the questions from Exercise 9.

> How much money do you save a month?

> I don't save any money. How much money do you save?

> I save a lot of money.

What We BUY

Conversation: Shopping time

3.06 1. **REAL TALK** Watch or listen to the teenagers. Check the things they spend money on.

- ☒ a video game
- ☐ birthday gifts for friends
- ☐ bus tickets
- ☒ clothes
- ☐ comic books
- ☒ food
- ☐ jewelry
- ☒ music
- ☒ plans with friends
- ☐ shoes
- ☐ sporting goods
- ☒ things for a cell phone

2. **YOUR TURN** How do *you* spend *your* money? Tell your partner.

3.07 3. Listen to Lisa talking with a store clerk. Complete the conversation.

USEFUL LANGUAGE: Making requests when shopping

| I'd like to buy | I'd prefer | I'll take it! | Can I try it on? |

Lisa: Excuse me. ¹_____ a dress.

Clerk: OK. How about this **blue dress**? It's new.

Lisa: ²_____ a different color. Does it come in **black**?

Clerk: Yes, it does. Here it is.

Lisa: Nice. How much is it?

Clerk: It's **$49**.

Lisa: ³_____

Clerk: Of course. What size do you wear?

Lisa: **Size 8**.

Clerk: OK. What do you think?

Lisa: Actually, it's not big enough. I need a larger size.

Clerk: OK. Try **a 10**. How is it?

Lisa: Great. ⁴_____

4. Practice the conversation with a partner.

5. **YOUR TURN** Repeat the conversation in Exercise 3, but change the words in purple. Use the information in the chart for one conversation and your own ideas for another.

		My ideas
Item	a sweater	
First color	red	
Second color	green	
Price	$35	
First size	a small	
Second size	a medium	

A WARM JACKET!

by Wayne, October 16
★★★★☆

The K-Light Jacket is a great jacket. The jacket is at Tom's Sporting Goods Store in a lot of colors. It costs $49.99. The jacket is **warm**, and it's good for hikes in cooler weather. It's not warm enough for very cold weather. Buy this jacket today. Wear it on your next hike! Note: Don't buy your usual size. I usually wear a medium, but I have this jacket in a large.

A TERRIBLE TABLET!

by Victoria, December 2
★☆☆☆☆

I'm writing this review about my new TS1 tablet. J & T Electronics sells it for $309.00. Don't buy this tablet! It's terrible. I work hard to earn my money, and this tablet isn't worth it. There is one good thing – the size. It's very small. But it's also very slow, and **sometimes it stops working**. You can't download many apps on the tablet. Save **your** money! Don't spend it on **this** awful product.

Reading to write: Product reviews

6. **Look at the reviews. Do you think the people like the products? Read the reviews to check.**

⊙ *Focus on* **CONTENT**
When you write a product review, include:
- the name of the product   - the price
- what you like about it   - what you don't like about it
- where you can buy it   - your recommendation

7. **Read Wayne's and Victoria's reviews again. Find examples for the categories in the Focus on Content box for each review.**

⊙ *Focus on* **LANGUAGE**
You can use the imperative to make recommendations. Use the base form of a verb for affirmative sentences. Use *don't* with the base form of a verb in negative sentences.
- ***Buy*** *this TV now!* ***Don't buy*** *that TV!*
- ***Get*** *the new Lazer cell phone today.* ***Don't get*** *the new Starz cell phone.*

8. **Find examples of imperatives in Wayne's and Victoria's reviews.**

9. **Put the words in the correct order to make sentences with the imperative. Write an affirmative and a negative sentence for each item.**

at home or work / use / this cell phone

1. _____

2. _____

on this book / money / spend

3. _____

4. _____

Writing: Your product review

◯ **PLAN**
Choose a product you have. Write notes about it.

Name	
Where to buy it	
Price	
What you like	
What you don't like	
Recommendation	

◯ **WRITE**
Write a review about the product. Use your notes to help you. Write at least 60 words.

◯ **CHECK**
Check your writing. Can you answer "yes" to these questions?

- Is information for each category from the Focus on Content box in your review?

- Do you use the imperative correctly?

ANIMAL

Students around the world are saving their money, and then they're saving animals!

One way students save an animal is to "adopt" one. This means students give money to an organization. The organization uses the students' money to help animals. The students get a photo of the animal and information about it. For example, some students adopt tigers. They give money to an organization that helps tigers in Asia. Other students adopt whales. They look at photos of whales online, and they choose a whale to help. The whales have names! Students get a photo of the whale, and they can also see how the whale is doing online.

Mrs. Monson's students are adopting an animal in another way. They're helping a cat without a home. Now, the cat is living in their classroom! Her name is Shadow. She eats a lot of food, and she needs to see a vet. The students are having a bake sale and selling cakes and cookies. They're using the money to feed and take care of Shadow. Shadow plays when the students are working! She sleeps in the classroom, too. At the end of the year, one student gets to keep Shadow!

Culture: Students helping animals

1. **Look at the photos. What animals do you see? Where do they live?**

2. **Read and listen to the article. What does it mean to adopt a pet?**

3. **Read the article again. Are the sentences *T* (true) or *F* (false)? Correct the false sentences.**

   1. An organization helps tigers in the United States. F ✓

   2. An organization helps whales in the ocean. T ✓

   3. The tigers have names. F ✓

   4. Students get a photo of the animal they help. T ✓

   5. Shadow is living at a school. T ✓

   6. Shadow doesn't eat enough food. F ✓

4. **YOUR TURN Work with a partner. Answer the questions.**

   1. Do you know anyone who earns or saves money to help people or animals? What do they do?

   2. How could you earn money to help people or animals? What people or animals would you help?

DID YOU KNOW...?

Many students in the United States have bake sales to earn money. They make food and sell it at school events. They spend the money on different things, like adopting an animal or buying sports uniforms.

BE CURIOUS

Find out about the number zero. Who created it? (Workbook, p. 77)

● **Discovery** EDUCATION

3.3 ZERO: PAST AND PRESENT

Vocabulary

1. Where do you buy or get these things? Label the pictures with the correct places.

a bank	a food court	a pharmacy
a bookstore	a music store	a sporting goods store

1. _a food count_   2. _a bank_

3. _a pharmacy_   4. _a music store_

5. _a bookstore_   6. _a sporting good store_

Grammar

2. Complete the sentences with the present continuous or simple present forms.

1. Kyle _drinks_ coffee at the café every morning.

2. What _are_ you usually _is_ at a department store?

3. Why _are_ they always _are_ money inside the bank instead of at an ATM?

4. Peter _celebra_ his birthday money right now.
   tes

3. Circle the correct answers.

1. There aren't **much** / **(many)** shoe stores at the mall.

2. Are there **much** / **(many)** watches at the jewelry store?

3. I don't have **some** / **(enough)** time to go to the ATM.

4. Do you want to eat **(some)** / **enough** food now?

Useful language

4. Complete the conversation with the correct sentences and phrases.

I'd like to buy	I'd prefer
I'll take them!	Can I try them on?

Jack: Hello. ¹ _I'd like to buy_ some new pants.

Clerk: OK. How about these blue pants?

Jack: ² _I'd prefer_ brown pants.

Clerk: OK. We have these in brown. What size do you need?

Jack: A medium, I think.
³ _Can I try them on?_

Clerk: Sure. Take a medium and a large. So, do you like them?

Jack: Yes, the medium pants are good.
⁴ _I'll take them_

PROGRESS CHECK: Now I can . . .

- ☑ identify places to shop.
- ☑ talk about the things I do every day and the things I'm doing now.
- ☐ ask and answer questions about spending and saving money.
- ☐ make requests when shopping.
- ☐ write a product review.
- ☐ talk about using money to help people or animals.

4 Our HEROES

Discovery
EDUCATION™

BE CURIOUS 🔒

Wildlife Hero

Who is your role model and why?

The Chilean Mine Rescue

Amelia Earhart: Famous Flyer

1. What are the people doing?

2. How do you think the boy feels about the man?

3. Who are some people you feel this way about?

UNIT CONTENTS

Vocabulary Cool jobs; adjectives of personality
Grammar Simple past statements review and *ago*; simple past questions review and *ago*
Listening Interview with a teenage hero

Vocabulary: Cool jobs

1. Label the pictures with the correct jobs.

an actor	a painter	a singer	✓ a writer
a dancer	a runner	a soccer player	
a lawyer	a scientist	a tennis player	

1. _a writer_ 2. _ʌ S P_ 3. _a s_ 4. _a d_ 5. _a P_

6. _a s_ 7. _a a_ 8. _a T_ 9. _a l_ 10. _a R_

2. Listen, check, and repeat.

3. Write the jobs in the correct places in the chart.

Sports	Arts and Entertainment		Academic
Runner	a writer	Painter	science
soccer	singer	dance	lawyer
tennis	actor	writer	

Speaking: Who does that job?

4. YOUR TURN Work with a partner. Can you think of a person (a family member, a friend, or a famous person) for each job?

> My uncle is a lawyer.   My mom is a lawyer, too.

5. Would you like these jobs? Why or why not?

> I'd like to be a writer. I want to write short stories.

> I wouldn't like to be a writer. I don't like to work alone.

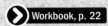
Workbook, p. 22

Say it RIGHT!

The letter *i* can make the short *i* sound /ɪ/. It can also make the long *i* sound /aɪ/. Listen to the sentence. The first *i* in *scientist* is long. The second *i* is short.

/aɪ/ /ɪ/
My parents are scientists.

Listen to the jobs again. Which other words have a short *i* (/ɪ/)? Which ones have a long *i* (/aɪ/)?

Reading Young and Talented!; My Hero; The Island of Champions
Conversation Asking for and giving clarification
Writing A description of a person you admire

SUPERSTARS

Young and Talented!

From sports and music to technology and film, today's stars are young and talented! These young people are at the top of their professions. Find out why!

Javier "Chicharito" Hernández was born in Guadalajara, Mexico. He started playing soccer when he was seven. At 15, he signed his first professional contract. In 2010, he moved to England to play for Manchester United. He won an award for Most Valuable Player (MVP) in 2011 when he was 23 years old. He now plays for both Manchester United and the Mexican national team.

Nick D'Aloisio was born in Australia, but he grew up in London, England. He got his first computer when he was nine, and he wrote his first app at 12. In 2013, at 17, he sold an app to Yahoo for 30 million dollars! He also got a job with the company.

Beyoncé won her first talent show when she was seven and joined her first band, Girl's Tyme, when she was eight. This band later became Destiny's Child. In 2001, she became a solo singer. She made her first solo album in 2003. She is now one of the best-paid singers in the world, and she also acts.

DID YOU KNOW...?

Talent often runs in the family. Javier Hernández's father and grandfather were professional soccer players. Beyoncé's sister is also a singer and actress.

Reading: A web page about young stars

1. **Look at the photos. Do you know these people? What are their jobs?**

2. **Read and listen to the article. At what age did each person take the first step to his or her future job? What was the first step?** (4.03)

3. **Read the article again. Complete the sentences with Nick D'Aloisio, Javier Hernández, or Beyoncé.**

   1. ___Javier___ and ___Beyonce___ won awards for their talents.
   2. ___N D'aloisio___ became a millionaire at age 17.
   3. ___Beyonce___ worked with a group and then worked alone.
   4. ___Javier___ and ___Beyounce___ moved to different countries.
   5. ___N D'aloisio___ got a job with a famous company.

4. **YOUR TURN Work with a partner. Think of a famous person from your country who is alive today. What does he or she do? What is he or she famous for?**

   > Diego Luna is a famous actor from Mexico City. He's famous for TV shows in Mexico and for movies in Mexico and in the United States.

Grammar: Simple past statements review and *ago*

5. Complete the chart.

Use simple past statements to describe things in the past and to talk about past events and activities. Use ago to say how far back in the past something happened or was.

	Affirmative statements	Negative statements
be	He _____ MVP in 2011. They **were** in Brazil a week **ago**.	He **wasn't** MVP in 2010. They **weren't** in Spain last week.
Regular verbs	He _____ for Mexico. I **moved** a month **ago**.	He **didn't play** for Spain. I _____ last week.
Irregular verbs	She _____ a solo album in 2003. I **got** a tablet a year _____.	She **didn't make** an album in 2001. I _____ a laptop.

Check your answers: Grammar reference, p. 109

Spell it RIGHT!

For regular verbs:

\+ **-ed**: work → work**ed**

\+ **-d**: live → live**d**

-y → **-i** + **-ed**: try → tr**ied**

double consonant + **-ed**: shop → shop**ped**

For irregular verbs: See p. 121.

6. Circle the correct words.

1. Gene Kelly (was) / **were** a famous dancer, actor, and singer.

2. I **wasn't** / **weren't** very good at singing when I **was** / **were** young.

3. You **wasn't** / **weren't** in class when the famous writer **was** / **were** there.

4. The Olympic runner **was** / **were** very tired after the race.

7. Rewrite the sentences in the simple past. Add the phrases in parentheses. The verbs in blue are irregular. Check the correct forms of those verbs on page 121.

1. John wants to be a professional tennis player. (10 years ago)

   John wanted to be a professional tennis player 10 years ago.

2. You write great short stories. (last year)

   _____

3. Lorena is getting a job as a lawyer. (last week)

   _____

4. I sing in a band. (in 2012)

   _____

5. The scientists don't work in the lab. (a week ago)

   _____

6. The runners are shopping for new shoes. (yesterday)

   _____

Get it RIGHT!

Remember that you do not add **-ed** to the end of irregular verbs in the simple past.

She **sang** alone. NOT: ~~She singed alone.~~

Speaking: Who is it?

8. YOUR TURN Think of a famous person. Write five facts about his/her life. Use the suggestions or your own ideas.

where he/she was born	when he/she became famous	an award he/she won
his/her job	how old he/she is	

9. Work with a group. Tell your group about your famous person. Can they guess who it is?

> She was born in Mexico. She is a singer, and she started singing when she was nine years old. She also acted in soap operas. She . . .

Is it Thalía?   Yes, it is!

Find out about a wildlife hero. What is her job? (Workbook, p. 78)

BE CURIOUS

Discovery EDUCATION

4.1 WILDLIFE HERO

Workbook, p. 23

Being BRAVE

Listening: Interview with a teenage hero

1. Did you see or help in an emergency in the past? What happened?

2. Listen to Marcos talk to a news reporter. What was the emergency? What did Marcos do?

3. Listen again and circle the correct answers.
   1. Marcos was **in his house** / outside when the fire started. ✓
   2. He saw **smoke** / **a strange light** in the sky. ✓
   3. Max was **in the house** / **outside**. ✗
   4. **Marcos** / Max's dad saw a ladder in the yard. ✓
   5. Marcos **broke** / **opened** the window. ✗
   6. Max climbed **down the ladder** / **into Marcos's arms**. ✓ ✗

Vocabulary: Adjectives of personality

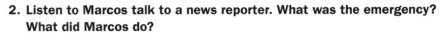

4. Match the pictures with the correct sentences. Then listen and check your answers.
   1. _a_ George is very **quiet**. He doesn't talk a lot.
   2. _f_ Katy's really **funny**. She makes me laugh a lot.
   3. _c_ Lou is very **serious**. He studies all the time.
   4. _e_ Martina's really **brave**. She isn't scared of anything!
   5. _b_ Leticia is so **cheerful**. She's so happy and always smiles.
   6. _h_ Julia was **calm** during the emergency. She didn't get excited, and she called the police right away.
   7. _d_ Brett is really **friendly**. He likes to meet new people.
   8. _i_ Tonya is very **kind** to animals. She helped a cat get down from a tree.
   9. _g_ Sometimes, Isabel is **stubborn**. She doesn't listen to her sister.

5. **YOUR TURN** Work with a partner. In what situations do the adjectives describe you?

> I'm calm and brave in an emergency. I'm usually friendly at parties. I'm . . .

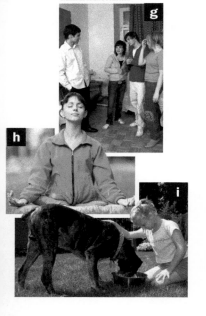

Grammar: Simple past questions review and *ago*

6. Complete the chart.

Use simple past questions to ask about past things, events, and activities.
Use ago to ask how far back in the past something happened or was.

	Wh- questions and answers	Yes/No questions and answers
be	How **was** he an hour _____? He **was** happy. Where **were** they? They _____ at home.	_____ he happy an hour **ago**? Yes, he **was**. / No, he **wasn't**. **Were** they at home? Yes, they _____. / No, they **weren't**.
Regular verbs	How long **ago did** it **start**? It **started** an hour **ago**. Why _____ you _____ him? I **carried** him because he was hurt.	**Did** it **start** an hour **ago**? Yes, it **did**. / No, it _____. _____ you **carry** him? Yes, I _____. / No, I **didn't**.
Irregular verbs	What _____ you _____? I **saw** a fire. Where **did** they **put** the ladder? They **put** it against the house.	**Did** you **see** a fire? Yes, I _____. / No, I **didn't**. **Did** they **put** the ladder against the house? Yes, they **did**. / No, they _____.

> Check your answers: Grammar reference, p. 109

7. Complete the sentences with the simple past forms of the verbs.

1. When __*were*__ you scared in the past? Why _____ you scared? (be)

2. _____ your friends ever _____ a fire? When _____ they _____ it? (see)

3. When _____ one of your friends brave? _____ you with him or her? (be)

4. _____ you _____ a stranger in the past? Who _____ you _____? (help)

8. Work with a partner. Ask and answer the questions in Exercise 7.

> When were you scared in the past? Why were you scared?

> I was scared last night. It was dark and stormy outside.

9. Complete the conversations with the simple past forms of the verbs.

| ✓ go | see | talk | think |

1. **A:** ___*Did*___ you ___*go*___ out last night?
   B: Yes, I did. I saw my cousin play tennis. She's a great tennis player.
2. **A:** Who _____ you _____ to at the party?
   B: To Sam and Patricia. They were very friendly.
3. **A:** _____ you _____ Carl in class?
   B: No, but I saw him about an hour ago. He was really cheerful.

Speaking: I was brave!

10. **YOUR TURN** Work with a partner. Ask and answer questions about a time you were brave. Use one of the suggestions or your own idea.

| you helped someone in danger | you did something you were afraid to do | you gave a presentation |

When were you brave? What happened? What did you do?

> When were you brave?

> I was brave last month. I went outside in the dark to find our cat.

People
WE ADMIRE

Conversation: Everyday heroes

))) 4.06

1. **REAL TALK** Watch or listen to the teenagers. Match the role models with the reasons.

1. Usain Bolt ___	a. saved his sister from a fire
2. big sister ___	b. helps children
3. Anne Hathaway ___	c. teaches well
4. grandfather ___	d. is the fastest runner in the world
5. a school friend ___	e. is nice, smart, and hardworking
6. history teacher ___	f. dances well

2. **YOUR TURN** Who is *your* role model and why? Tell your partner.

))) 4.07

3. Listen to Darren and Lydia talking about heroes. Complete the conversation.

> **USEFUL LANGUAGE: Asking for and giving clarification**
>
> Are you saying that   What do you mean?   What I'm trying to say is that   I mean

Darren: We talked about heroes in class today.

Lydia: That's interesting.

Darren: Yeah, but I didn't agree with most of the people in the class.

Lydia: Really? ¹_____

Darren: Most people chose **movie stars**. I don't think they're heroes.

Lydia: ²_____ celebrities can't be heroes?

Darren: Well, they can be, but maybe they shouldn't be. ³_____, **acting** isn't heroic.

Lydia: But a lot of **movie stars** help people.

Darren: Yes, but most celebrities help people *after* they're famous. ⁴_____ I think everyday people are more heroic.

Lydia: Oh, I see. So, who is your hero?

Darren: **My Aunt Karin. She started a rescue center for wild animals.**

Lydia: Well, that is pretty heroic!

4. Practice the conversation with a partner.

5. **YOUR TURN** Repeat the conversation in Exercise 3, but change the words in purple. Use the information in the chart for one conversation and your own ideas for another.

		My ideas
Type of hero the class chose	pop star	
Activity	singing	
Darren's/your hero	grandfather	
Reason	He fights for peace.	

MY HERO by Gloria Marconi

My hero is **Captain Sullenberger**. He is famous because he saved the lives of many people. In 2009, he was the pilot on a flight from **New York City**. The airplane engines stopped working. Captain Sullenberger stayed calm and landed the plane in the **Hudson River**. After 2009, he wrote two books about being brave.

I admire Captain Sullenberger due to his heroic act. I also admire him because he is serious about safety. Now he is a **safety expert**, and he gives people and companies advice about being safe. He's also kind and teaches children about aviation and safety. Since he's a good role model, he is my **hero**!

Reading to write: Gloria's hero

6. **Look at the photos in Gloria's text. What job does her hero have? Why is he a hero? Read the description to check.**

> **◉ Focus on CONTENT**
> When you write about someone you admire, include this information:
> - who he/she is and his/her job
> - heroic things he/she did or does
> - his/her personality
> - why you admire him/her

7. **Read Gloria's description again. What information from the Focus on Content box does she include?**

> **◉ Focus on LANGUAGE**
> **Connectors to show reasons: *because, since, due to***
> Use a subject and a verb after ***because*** and ***since***.
> The clause with ***because*** or ***since*** can be at the beginning or end of a sentence.
> *I admire my mother **because** she works very hard.*
> ***Since** my aunt helps animals, she's my role model.*
> Use a noun after ***due to***. The clause with ***due to*** can be at the beginning or end of a sentence.
> *Nelson Mandela was famous **due to** his fight for peace.*
> ***Due to** his fight for peace, Nelson Mandela was famous.*

8. **Find examples of *because*, *since*, and *due to* in Gloria's description.**

9. **Circle the correct word or phrase.**

   1. My cousin Lou was Player of the Year **because / due to** his skills.

   2. **Because / Due to** Jenny is kind, we admire her.

   3. Painters Frida Kahlo and Diego Rivera were even more famous **since / due to** they were married to each other.

   4. J. K. Rowling is a well-known writer **since / due to** her Harry Potter series.

 Writing: Your hero

◯ PLAN
First, choose a person you admire. It can be a famous person or someone you know. Use the categories in the Focus on Content box and take notes.

Who he/she is and his/her job	
Heroic things he/she did or does	
His/Her personality	
Why you admire him/her	

◯ WRITE
Now, write about the person you admire. Use your notes to help you. Write at least 60 words.

◯ CHECK
Check your writing. Can you answer "yes" to these questions?

- Is information for each category from the Focus on Content box in your description?

- Do you use connectors to show reasons correctly?

The Island of CHAMPIONS

Only about three million people live in Jamaica, a small Caribbean island, but many famous athletes are from this country. Athletics is an important part of life in Jamaica, and its athletes are national heroes. Most elementary schools have sports programs, and many high school students compete in an athletics championship, or "Champs," in Kingston every year. Many of the schoolchildren are Olympic champions of the future.

Jamaica's first Olympic heroes were Arthur Wint and Herb McKenley. They won gold and silver medals in the men's 400m race in 1948. From that moment, Jamaican athletics became a national obsession. In 1980, at the Moscow Olympics, Merlene Ottey became the first Jamaican woman to win a medal. She won bronze in the 200m race. She won eight more Olympic medals over 20 years, including two in the 2000 Sydney Olympics at age 40!

In 2008, in Beijing, a new hero won the men's 100m and 200m Olympic gold medals: Usain Bolt. In the London Olympics, in 2012, he became the first athlete to win the "double-double" when he won gold medals in both races again. Jamaican Yohan Blake won silver in both of those races. Shelly-Ann Fraser-Pryce won the gold in the women's 100m and silver in the 200m, bringing home two more medals for Team Jamaica. In fact, Jamaica dominated the medals list in the 2012 Olympics. They won 12 medals, all in track and field events. Jamaica really is the home of champions!

Culture: Athletes from Jamaica

1. **Look at the photos. Which country do you think the article is about? Do you know who the runners are?**

2. **Read and listen to the article. Circle the main idea.**
   a. Jamaican high school students are heroes.
   b. Jamaican men and women are equally good at athletics.
   c. There are many Olympic champions from Jamaica.

3. **Read the article again. Are the sentences true or false? Write T (true), F (false), or NI (no information).**
   1. Jamaica is unusual because it's small, but many athletic champions are from there. _T_
   2. Arthur Wint and Herb McKenley were the only Jamaican athletes to win a medal in the 1948 Olympics. _F_
   3. Merlene Ottey's first Olympic medal was gold. _NI_
   4. Usain Bolt won both the 100m and 200m races in Beijing and London. _T_

4. **YOUR TURN** **Work with a partner. Make a list of famous athletes from your country. Why do people admire them?**

   > Lorena Ochoa is famous because she was one of the top female golfers in the world.

   > Yes, and people admire her because she started a golfing school for people in Mexico.

DID YOU KNOW...?

Over 30,000 people go to "Champs" to watch the athletes. Many young runners break national records at the championship.

BE CURIOUS — Find out about a mine accident and rescue. How many people were in the mine? (Workbook, p. 79)

DISCOVERY EDUCATION

4.3 THE CHILEAN MINE RESCUE

Vocabulary

1. Label the pictures with the correct jobs.

1. _Bussines man_ 2. _Tennis player_

3. _Scientifist_ 4. _Painter_

2. Complete the sentences with the correct adjectives.

cheerful	funny	serious	kind

1. My brother isn't good at telling jokes. He's not very _funny_.

2. Martin is always telling jokes. He's not very _serious_.

3. Jacquelyn doesn't smile or laugh very often. She's not very _cheerful_.

4. Liz and Josh help kids with their homework after school. They're very _kind_.

Grammar

3. Circle the correct words.

1. Where **were** / **did** you last weekend?

2. **Were** / **Did** you play sports in high school?

3. **Was** / **Did** Mike a fast runner as a child?

4. **Were** / **Did** your parents at home last night?

4. Complete the sentences with the simple past. Then rewrite the sentences with the correct time periods and *ago*.

1. I _had_ (have) lunch at 1:00 p.m. Now it's 2:00 p.m.

   I had lunch an hour ago.

2. Jack ⁓ (start) school on Monday. Today is Thursday.

   Jack started school on Monday

3. I ⁓ (call) you at 9:15 a.m. Now it's 9:20 a.m.

   I called you at 9:15 a.m.

4. Marcos ⁓ (be) Most Valuable Player in March. Now it's April.

   Marcos be. most Valudbb player

Useful language

5. Complete the conversations with the correct phrases.

Are you saying that	I mean
What do you mean?	What I'm trying to say is that

Kim: I think athletes are overpaid.

Todd: ¹ _What I'm trying to say is that_

Kim: ² _Are you saying_, they make too much money.

Luke: My brother is the fastest runner in the world!

Sara: ³ _What do you_ he runs faster than Usain Bolt?

Luke: No. ⁴ _I mean_ he runs really fast!

PROGRESS CHECK: Now I can . . .

- ☐ identify some cool jobs.
- ☐ share facts about someone's life.
- ☐ ask and answer questions about being brave.
- ☐ ask for and give clarification.
- ☐ write a description of someone I admire.
- ☐ talk about famous athletes from my country.

▶ REVIEW UNITS 3–4, Workbook, pp. 28–29

CLIL PROJECT

4.4 Amelia Earhart: Famous Flyer, p. 117

5 *It's a* Mystery!

Discovery
EDUCATION

BE CURIOUS 🔒

Mysteries in the Mountains

What's an unusual or interesting thing that happened to you recently?

The Case of the Missing Woman

An Underwater Mystery

1. Who do you think made these statues on Easter Island?

2. Why do you think people made them?

3. Do you know of any mysterious things or places? Where are they?

UNIT CONTENTS

Vocabulary   Action verbs; adverbs of manner
Grammar   Past continuous; adverbs of time; simple past vs. past continuous; *when* and *while*
Listening   I saw something strange last night.

Vocabulary: Action verbs

1. Look at the pictures of a police officer's story.
   Match the sentences with the pictures.

a. I **caught** the thief after he fell.

b. I **chased** the thief down the street.

c. The thief **climbed** the wall.

d. The thief **hid** the bag.

e. The thief **fell** on the ground.

f. The thief **jumped** into someone's yard.

✓ g. The thief **stole** a bag and **ran** by my police car.

h. The thief **threw** the bag over a wall.

2. Listen, check, and repeat.

3. Work with a partner. One person is a reporter and the other is the police officer. Ask and answer questions for each event in the story in Exercise 1.

> What did the thief steal?

> Where did he run?

> He stole a bag.

> He ran by my . . .

Speaking: What can you . . . ?

4. **YOUR TURN** Work with a partner. Think of as many answers as you can for each question. Make a list.

   What can you . . .

   1. catch?   2. chase?   3. climb?   4. hide?   5. jump over?   6. throw?

   > catch – a thief, a basketball, a baseball, a bus, a cold . . .

5. Join another pair. Compare your lists.

▶ Workbook, p. 30

Reading Whodunit?; An Urban Legend; The World's Number One Detective
Conversation Telling and reacting to a story
Writing A narrative about an interesting or unusual event

Solving MYSTERIES

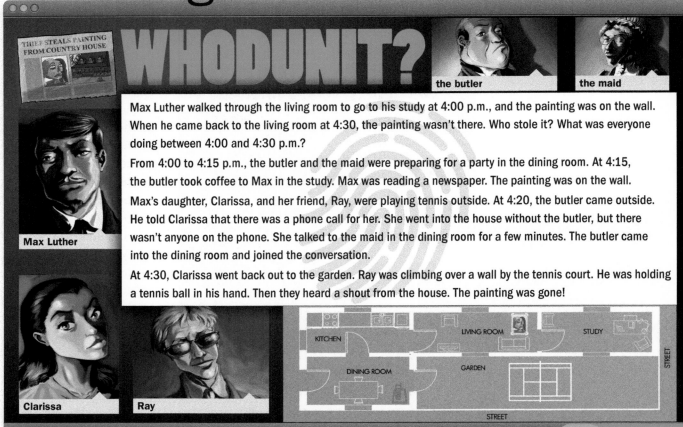

WHODUNIT?

the butler | the maid

Max Luther walked through the living room to go to his study at 4:00 p.m., and the painting was on the wall. When he came back to the living room at 4:30, the painting wasn't there. Who stole it? What was everyone doing between 4:00 and 4:30 p.m.?

From 4:00 to 4:15 p.m., the butler and the maid were preparing for a party in the dining room. At 4:15, the butler took coffee to Max in the study. Max was reading a newspaper. The painting was on the wall.

Max's daughter, Clarissa, and her friend, Ray, were playing tennis outside. At 4:20, the butler came outside. He told Clarissa that there was a phone call for her. She went into the house without the butler, but there wasn't anyone on the phone. She talked to the maid in the dining room for a few minutes. The butler came into the dining room and joined the conversation.

At 4:30, Clarissa went back out to the garden. Ray was climbing over a wall by the tennis court. He was holding a tennis ball in his hand. Then they heard a shout from the house. The painting was gone!

Reading: An article about a stolen painting

1. **Look at the pictures. What was the crime? Where did it happen?**

5.02
2. **Read and listen to the crime story. Who do you think stole the painting? How do you think it happened?**

3. **Read the article again and answer the questions.**

   1. Where was the painting?

      Living room

   2. What time did the painting disappear?

      4:15 and 4:30

   3. Why were the butler and maid in the dining room?

      a party

   4. Why did Clarissa go into the house?

      a phone call

   5. What did Ray lose behind the wall?

      a tennis ball

4. **Work with a partner. Who stole the painting? Explain your idea. Then check your idea on page 121.**

5. **YOUR TURN Work with a small group. Do you know any other stories about a thief (real or fictional)? What did the thief steal? Did the police catch him or her?**

> There was a famous bank robbery last year. The thief stole $500,000. The police . . .

Grammar: Past continuous

6. Complete the chart.

Use the past continuous to talk about activities that were in progress in the past.

Wh- questions	Affirmative answers	Negative answers
What _____ you **doing**?	I **was talking** on the phone.	I **wasn't talking** to Max.
What **was** Max **reading**?	He **was reading** a newspaper.	He _____ **reading** a book.
What **were** they **doing**?	They _____ **playing** tennis.	They **weren't playing** soccer.

Yes/No questions	Short answers	
Were you **talking** to Max?	Yes, I **was**.	No, I **wasn't**.
Was Max **reading**?	Yes, he _____.	No, he **wasn't**.
_____ they **playing** tennis?	Yes, they **were**.	No, they _____.

> Check your answers: Grammar reference, p. 110

7. Complete the police report with the past continuous.

POLICE REPORT   CASE NO: 76543

Police officer: Alfred Baker   Name of witness: Jim Hanson   Crime: Stolen bike

Q: What ¹ _____were_____ you _____doing_____ (do) at the time?

A: My friends and I ² _____ (play) in the park. I ³ _____ (stand) on a hill.
  From there, I saw the thief steal the bike.

Q: What ⁴ _____ the thief _____ (wear)?

A: He ⁵ _____ (wear) a blue jacket and jeans.

Q: ⁶ _____ your friends _____ (watch) the thief?

A: No, they ⁷ _____. They ⁸ _____ (ride) their skateboards. They didn't see him.

8. Put the words in the correct order to make questions. Then answer the questions with your own information.

yesterday at 8:00 a.m. / you / what / were / doing

1. *What were you doing yesterday at 8:00 a.m.?*

2. *I was* _____

doing / were / last Saturday at 2:00 p.m. / your friends / what

3. _____

4. _____

Speaking: What were you doing?

9. **YOUR TURN** Work with a partner. Think of something you were doing at one of these times. Give your partner clues. Your partner guesses.

yesterday at 12:00 p.m.	last night
last Saturday afternoon	last Friday at 2:00 p.m.

> I was sitting in a stadium and watching something last Saturday afternoon.

> Were you watching a soccer game?

> Yes, I was.

Adverbs of time

Use adverbs of time to say when things happened or were happening at a specific time in the past.

this morning/afternoon; yesterday
last night/Monday/weekend/week/month/year
at 2:00 p.m./4:00 p.m./10:00 p.m.

Say it RIGHT!

In the word **was**, the **a** makes the short /u/ sound, and the **s** makes the /z/ sound. Listen to the sentences.
*What **was** she doing yesterday afternoon? She **was** playing tennis.*
Pay attention to your pronunciation of **was** in Exercise 8.

Find out about an archeological dig in Bolivia. What did Scotty and his team find out about the bones? (Workbook, p. 80)

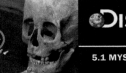

5.1 MYSTERIES IN THE MOUNTAINS

> Workbook, p. 31

Unsolved MYSTERIES

Listening: I saw something strange last night.

1. Did you see or read about something you couldn't explain in the past? What was it?

2. Listen to Kati tell Todd about an unexplained event. What did she see?

3. Listen again. Who did it? Write *K* for Kati or *T* for Todd.

1. was at home last night _____

2. was watching TV last night _____

3. was studying last night _____

4. is going to watch the sky tonight _____

Vocabulary: Adverbs of manner

4. Look at the pictures and the boldfaced words. These words are adverbs. You can form adverbs from adjectives. Complete the sentences with the correct adverbs. Then listen and check your answers.

quick → **quickly**	bad → **badly**
slow → **slowly**	happy → **happily**
loud → **loudly**	terrible → **terribly** ✓
quiet → **quietly**	hard → **hard**
careful → **carefully**	good → **well**

> **Spell it RIGHT!**
>
> To change an adjective to an adverb:
> - change *-y* to *-i* and add *-ly*:
>   happy → happ**ily**
> - change *-ble* to *-bly*:
>   terrib**le** → terrib**ly**

1. Gina slept ___*terribly*___ last night.

2. The dog barked _____.

3. The snail was moving _____.

4. The archaeologist worked with the bones _____.

5. Richard plays the piano _____.

6. The plane flew by _____.

7. Carlos sings _____.

8. The children were playing _____.

9. We entered the room _____.

5. **YOUR TURN** Work with a partner. Ask and answer questions using the adverbs in Exercise 4. Use the words below or your own ideas.

☐ catch a ball	☐ clean your bedroom	☐ play tennis	☐ sing
☐ check your homework	☐ cook	☐ run	☐ throw a ball

Do you run quickly?

No, I don't. I run slowly.

Grammar: Simple past vs. past continuous; *when* and *while*

6. Complete the chart.

> *Use the past continuous for an event that was in progress.*
> *Use the simple past for an event that interrupted the event in progress.*
> *Use* when *or* while *with the phrase in the past continuous.*
> *Use* when *with the phrase in the simple past.*

> I _____ **studying** when I **saw** red lights in the sky.
> (event in progress)   (event that interrupts)

> While/When I **was studying**, I _____ red lights in the sky.
> (event in progress)   (event that interrupts)

> **When** it **happened**, my parents _____ **sleeping**.
> (event that interrupts)   (event in progress)

> It _____ **while/when** my parents **were sleeping**.
> (event that interrupts)   (event in progress)

> Check your answers: Grammar reference, p. 110

7. Circle *when* or *while*. Sometimes both answers are possible.

1. Karl caught the ball (**when**) / (**while**) Sandra was running.

2. Olivia was practicing the piano **when** / **while** the phone rang.

3. I heard the loud sound **when** / **while** I was cleaning my room.

4. **When** / **While** the police officer was chasing the thief, he fell.

5. **When** / **While** someone knocked on the door, I was watching TV.

8. Complete the sentences with the simple past or past continuous.

1. Janet watched a mystery movie while she ___was eating___ (eat) dinner.

2. I was running in the park when I _____ (see) a police officer.

3. When the lights _____ (go) out, Doug was working.

4. When the fire alarm rang, you _____ (take) a test.

5. While the cat _____ (hide) under the bed, we heard her meow.

Speaking: While you were . . .

9. **YOUR TURN** Work with a partner. Talk about things that happened while you were doing some of these things in the past.

| cooking | eating | exercising | sleeping | studying |

> My phone rang while I was sleeping last night.

> Really? When I was sleeping, I had a nightmare.

10. **YOUR TURN** Join another pair. Tell the pair two things that happened to your partner.

> Last night, Jake had a nightmare while he was sleeping.

Get it **RIGHT!**

Use the simple past, not the past continuous, for an event that interrupts an event in progress.
Our team was playing well when I **scored** *a goal.*
NOT: ~~Our team was playing well when I~~ ~~**was scoring** a goal.~~

NOTICE IT
A *nightmare* is a very bad dream.

Workbook, pp. 32-33

Unit 5 | **47**

Strange STORIES

Conversation: An unusual dream

 5.06

1. Watch or listen to the teenagers. Circle the correct words.

1. The boy's soccer team (won) / **lost** the game.

2. The girl's cat (**chased**) / **ran toward** her.

3. (**The girl**) / **The teacher** gave the class some chocolate for her birthday.

4. Two girls **wore** / (**gave each other**) the same shirt.

5. Someone (**made**) / **took** the boy's lunch at school.

6. Someone stole the boy's **bike** / (**lock**).

2. YOUR TURN What's an unusual or interesting thing that happened to *you* recently? Tell your partner.

 5.07

3. Dave is telling Anna about a nightmare. Listen and complete the conversation with the words from the box.

> **USEFUL LANGUAGE: Telling and reacting to a story**
>
> then what happened | Did I tell you about | That's weird! | In the beginning

Dave: ¹ _Did I tell you about_ my dream last night?

Anna: No. Tell me about it.

Dave: OK. ² _In the begging_ , I was **in a park** at night. I was **walking slowly** when a **bear** jumped out at me!

Anna: Oh, no! What did you do?

Dave: I hid behind **a big tree**, and I waited quietly. But **the tree** got smaller and smaller!

Anna: ³ _Thats weird!_

Dave: I know. Then the **bear** found me and chased me! While the **bear** was chasing me, I **screamed loudly**!

Anna: So, ⁴ _the what happened_ ?

Dave: The **bear** caught me, and I woke up! It was scary!

4. Practice the conversation with a partner.

5. YOUR TURN Repeat the conversation in Exercise 3, but change the words in purple. Use the information in the chart for one conversation and your own ideas for another.

		My ideas
Place	on a street	on a forest
First action	riding my bike quickly	hide myself
Animal	dragon	Tiger
Hiding place	a car	a rock
Second action	threw my jacket at it	Throw a rock

to distract him

AN URBAN LEGEND

by Stacy Meyers

"Oh, no! I have to help," thought Mickey. One day last summer, he was driving slowly along a quiet road when he saw a car next to the road. A man had a flat tire, and he was trying to change it. Mickey stopped his car and helped the man. While they were changing the tire, they talked about their families. Then the man asked Mickey for his address. At first, Mickey said no, but the man asked him again and again, so Mickey gave it to him. One week later, Mickey got a letter:

> Dear Mickey,
> Thanks for your help. I know a lot about computers but nothing about cars!
> Bill Gates

Finally, Mickey knew who the man was – the founder of one of the world's largest computer companies. He was also one of the richest people in the world. And there was a check for $10,000 with the letter!

Reading to write: A narrative about an unusual event

6. **Look at the illustration. What do you think happened? Read Stacy's story to check.**

⦿ *Focus on* **CONTENT**

When you write a story, include:
- a beginning: It should get the readers' attention and make them want to read more.
- a middle: It has details about the events and is in chronological order.
- an ending: It brings the story to a close. A story can have a surprise ending.

7. **Read Stacy's story again. What gets the readers' attention at the beginning? What is the surprise ending?**

⦿ *Focus on* **LANGUAGE**

Sequencing words

Use sequencing words to:
- start a story: ***One day/night/time, . . . In the beginning, . . .***
- order events: ***At first, . . . Next, . . . Then . . .***
        After that, . . . Ten minutes later, . . .
- end a story: ***In the end, . . . Finally, . . .***

8. **Find examples of sequencing words in Stacy's story.**

9. **Complete the story with the correct words.**

at first	finally	later	one night	then

¹_____, I was doing my homework quietly in my bedroom when I heard a strange noise outside. ²_____, I didn't want to go outside, but ³_____ I opened the door, and I went into the yard. There was a very small dog, and it was barking loudly. While I was playing with the dog, my mom came home. She was laughing. Five minutes ⁴_____, my dad and sister arrived. They were laughing, too. ⁵_____, I understood. The dog was my birthday present!

Writing: Your narrative

◯ **PLAN**

Think of an interesting or unusual story. It can be something that really happened, or you can create the story. Write notes about the events in the order they happened.

Beginning:	_____
Middle:	_____
	_____
	_____
Ending:	_____

◯ **WRITE**

Write your story. Use your notes to help you. Write at least 80 words.

◯ **CHECK**

Check your writing. Can you answer "yes" to these questions?

- Does your story have a beginning, a middle, and an ending? Are the events in chronological order?

- Do you use sequencing words correctly?

▶ Workbook, pp. 34–35

The World's Number One
DETECTIVE

A Sherlock Holmes is famous for solving impossible crimes carefully and easily. He lived at 221B Baker Street in London. He played the violin well and was good at science. He didn't really exist, but he became famous in England more than 125 years ago, and he's famous all over the world today.

B Scottish writer Sir Arthur Conan Doyle wrote the original Sherlock Holmes stories. The first story appeared in a British magazine in 1887. It was the first of 56 stories. Doyle also wrote four Sherlock Holmes books. Doyle was working as a doctor when he wrote the first stories. He often wrote the stories while he was waiting for his patients.

C The detective's assistant, Dr. Watson, is almost as famous as Holmes, and the two always worked together. Holmes liked to explain the crimes to Watson. In the movies, Holmes answers Watson's questions with the phrase, "Elementary, my dear Watson, elementary," which means, "The answer is easy." But Holmes never really said this in any of the original stories or books.

D There are more than 200 Sherlock Holmes movies and TV shows with many different actors playing the roles of Holmes and Watson. In a recent TV series, *Elementary*, the stories take place today. Holmes lives in New York City, and his assistant, Dr. Watson, is a woman.

E Sherlock Holmes is everywhere! There are Sherlock Holmes games, toys, hats, comic books, and video games. There's even a Sherlock Holmes social networking page!

Culture: Sherlock Holmes

1. **Look at the photos. What do you know about Sherlock Holmes? What can you tell about him from the photos?**

2. **Read and listen to the article. Match the paragraphs (A–E) to the topics.**

   1. Holmes in Today's Culture ____

   2. Partners in Crime ____

   3. Holmes in Movies and on TV ____

   4. Fame: Past and Present ____

   5. Sherlock Holmes Stories ____

3. **Read the article again. Circle the correct answers.**

   1. Sherlock Holmes was **a real** / **an imaginary** detective.

   2. The writer of Sherlock Holmes was a **doctor** / **detective**.

   3. In the **movies** / **books**, Holmes's famous phrase is "Elementary, my dear Watson, elementary."

   4. There are about **125** / **200** Sherlock Holmes movies and TV shows.

4. **YOUR TURN** **Work with a partner. Are there any famous fictional characters in your country? Who are they and what do they do?**

   > Pascualina is a famous fictional character. There are many books about her. She travels around the world and . . .

BE CURIOUS

DID YOU KNOW . . . ?
Sherlock Holmes died in one of Doyle's stories in 1893, but the writer brought him back to life because his fans got angry!

Find out about a young woman who disappears from her home. What happened to her? (Workbook, p. 81)

Discovery EDUCATION

5.3 THE CASE OF THE MISSING WOMAN

UNIT 5 REVIEW

Vocabulary

1. Match the phrases to make sentences.

1. A police officer chased the thief ____
2. The thief threw ____
3. Then he jumped ____
4. The thief hid ____

a. his bag into the river.
b. at his friend's house until the police officer finally found him.
c. into the river and swam away.
d. down the street for 2 kilometers.

2. Complete the sentences with the correct adverbs of manner.

1. Carlos slept _____ (terrible) because of the storm.
2. My brother sat _____ (quiet) and watched his favorite Sherlock Holmes movie.
3. The detective studied the crime scene _____ (careful).
4. He worked _____ (hard) to solve the crime.

Grammar

3. Look at Gabe's calendar. Write sentences in the past continuous about what he was doing.

Monday
1 8:00 p.m.
shop for mom's birthday present

Wednesday
3 4:00 p.m.
watch a soccer game with brother

Friday
12 8:00 a.m – 4:00 p.m. clean the garage
8:00 p.m. hang out at a café with friend

1. (last Monday night)

_____

_____

2. (last Wednesday afternoon) _____

_____

3. (Friday evening) _____

_____

4. Write sentences using the simple past and past continuous.

1. he / answer / the phone / while / he / eat / dinner

_____

2. we / have / a picnic / when / it / start / to rain

_____

3. Mark / not wear / a helmet / when / he / fall / off his bike

_____

Useful language

5. Complete the conversation with the correct phrases.

then what happened	Did I tell you about	That's weird.	In the beginning

Elsa: Hey, Ned. ¹_____ my vacation?

Ned: No, you didn't. Did you have a good time?

Elsa: ²_____, I had a great time. But then my bag was stolen at a restaurant.

Ned: Oh, no!

Elsa: Oh, yes! I put my bag on the back of my chair while I was eating. I didn't even see it happen.

Ned: ³_____

Elsa: I know. Luckily, a police officer was sitting next to me. She saw and chased the thief!

Ned: So, ⁴_____?

Elsa: She caught the thief and gave me back my bag!

PROGRESS CHECK: Now I can . . .

- ☐ tell a story with action verbs.
- ☐ talk about what I was doing in the past.
- ☐ talk about past events and describe how I do things.
- ☐ tell an interesting or unusual story.
- ☐ write a story about an interesting or unusual event.
- ☐ understand information and talk about fictional characters.

CLIL PROJECT

5.4 An Underwater Mystery, p. 118

UNITS 1–5 Review Game

TEAM 1
START

In one minute, name a modern example and a traditional example of something for each of these categories: food, music, and sports.

Ask a teammate about someone he or she knows. Ask two Wh- questions and two Yes/No questions. Your teammate answers.

Talk with a teammate about traditions in your families, such as birthdays or weddings. See how long you can keep the conversation going by asking and answering questions.

In one minute, name as many types of movies as you can.

Ask a teammate five questions about people's possessions in the classroom. Use whose. Your teammate answers.

In one minute, name five different characters or actors from five different types of TV shows.

Make five statements about your movie-watching habits using the adverbs of frequency: always, usually, often, sometimes, and never.

Role-play a conversation with a teammate about a sports team or sporting event. Keep the conversation going for two minutes.

You want to go shopping at the mall. Ask a teammate where to buy three different things. Your teammate answers the questions.

Look around the room. Tell a teammate five things you see happening right now.

Ask a teammate for his/her opinion about three different TV shows. Disagree with your teammate's opinions.

INSTRUCTIONS:
- Make teams and choose game pieces.
- Put your game pieces on your team's START.
- Flip a coin to see who goes first.
- Read the first challenge. Can you do it correctly?

  Yes → Continue to the next challenge.

  No → Lose your turn.

The first team to do all of the challenges wins!

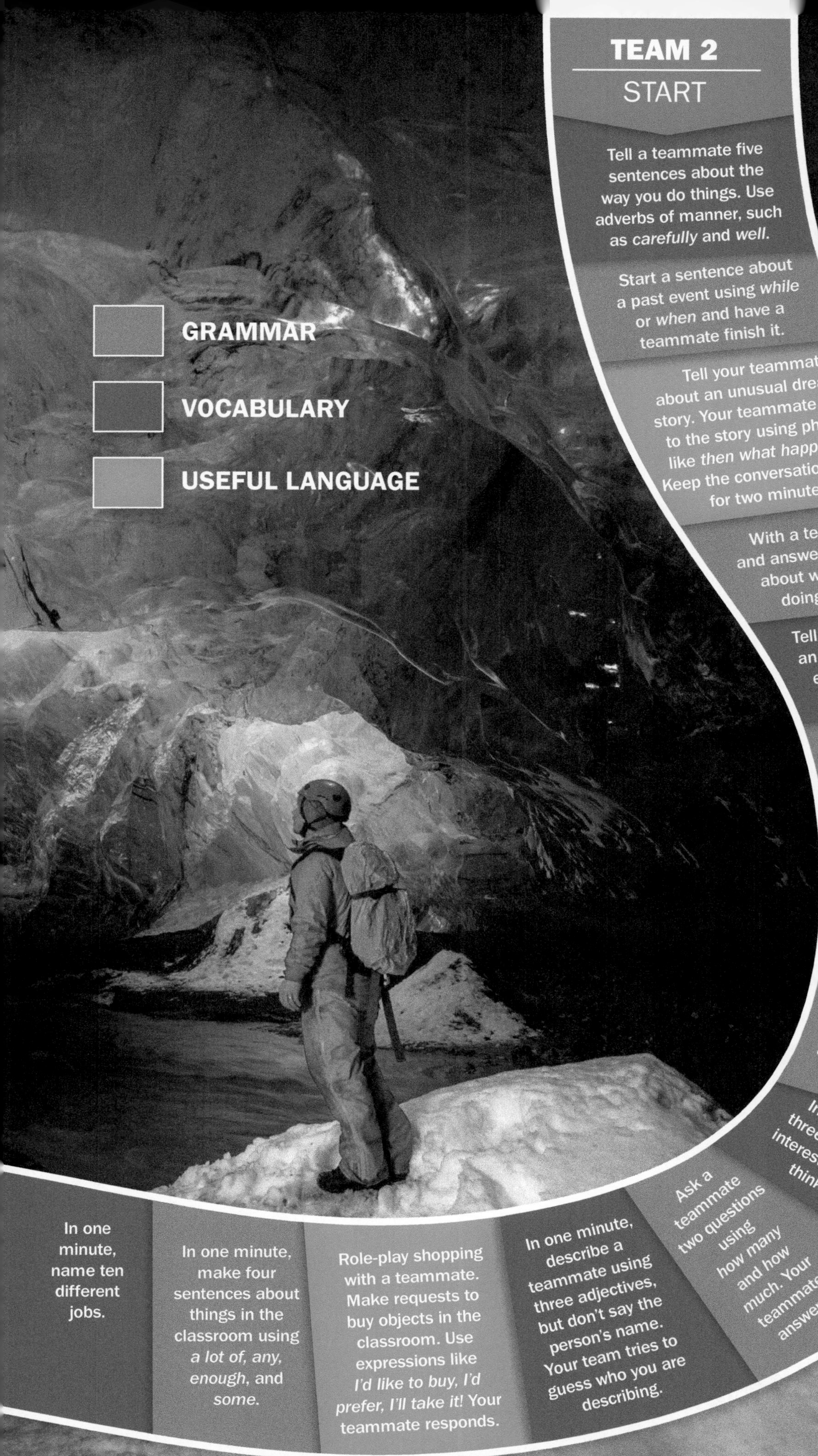

☐ **GRAMMAR**

☐ **VOCABULARY**

☐ **USEFUL LANGUAGE**

Tell a teammate five sentences about the way you do things. Use adverbs of manner, such as *carefully* and *well*.

Start a sentence about a past event using *while* or *when* and have a teammate finish it.

Tell your teammate about an unusual dream or story. Your teammate reacts to the story using phrases like *then what happened?* Keep the conversation going for two minutes.

With a teammate, ask and answer four questions about what you were doing last night.

Tell a teammate the story of an action movie or sporting event using at least four action verbs.

Ask your teammate *Wh-* questions and *Yes/No* questions to find out about a time in the past when he or she was brave or helpful. Your teammate answers.

Tell a teammate about one of your heroes. Your teammate asks questions for clarification.

Tell a teammate three things about yourself that happened in the past. Use *ago* to say how far back in the past.

In one minute, name three jobs you think are interesting and three you think are boring.

Ask a teammate two questions using *how many* and *how much.* Your teammate answers.

In one minute, describe a teammate using three adjectives, but don't say the person's name. Your team tries to guess who you are describing.

Role-play shopping with a teammate. Make requests to buy objects in the classroom. Use expressions like *I'd like to buy, I'd prefer, I'll take it!* Your teammate responds.

In one minute, make four sentences about things in the classroom using *a lot of, any, enough,* and *some.*

In one minute, name ten different jobs.

6 Home, Sweet HOME

1. What is this house like?

2. Who do you think lives here?

3. Would you want to live in a house like this? Why or why not?

UNIT CONTENTS

Vocabulary Furniture and other household items; household appliances

Grammar Comparative and superlative adjectives swed adverbs; *should* (*not*), (*not*) *have to*, *must* (*not*)

Listening A clothing emergency

Vocabulary: Furniture and other household items

1. Match the words with the correct pictures.

a. a bed   c. a chair   e. a dresser   g. a shower   i. a table   ✓k. an armchair

b. a bookcase   d. a desk   f. a mirror   h. a sofa   j. a toilet   l. cabinets

LIVING ROOM   **KITCHEN**   **BEDROOM**   **BATHROOM**

1. k ✓   2. b ✓   3. h ✓   4. i ✓   5. L ✓   6. C ✓   7. a ✓   8. d ✓   9. e ✓   10. f ✓   11. j ✓   12. g ✓

 2. Listen, check, and repeat.

3. Answer the questions with the words in Exercise 1.

1. Which items do you sit on?

   Chair, Sofa and bed

2. Which items do you put things in?

   Bookcase, desk and cabinets

3. Which items do you put things on?

   Table, desk, bed.

4. Which items do you get into?

   Bed, shower.

5. Which item do you look into?

   MIRROR, cabinets

 Say it RIGHT!

The letters **er** and **or** can make the /ər/ sound. Listen to the sentence.

*A photo of an act**or** is ov**er** my bed.*

Listen to the words in Exercise 1 again. Which words have the /ər/ sound? What letters make the sound?

4. Work with a partner. Describe the furniture and items in Exercise 1.

> The armchair is big. It's brown and blue.

Speaking: Your house

5. **YOUR TURN** Which things from Exercise 1 are in your house? What other things do you have? Make a list.

> *Kitchen: cabinets, two chairs, . . .*

6. Work with a partner. Tell your partner about the things in your house.

> There isn't a table in our kitchen. There are a lot of cabinets. We have two chairs by the window . . .

 Workbook, p. 36

Reading A Home in the Jungle; My House; Life on the Water
Conversation Asking for and offering help
Writing An email about your house

UNUSUAL Rooms

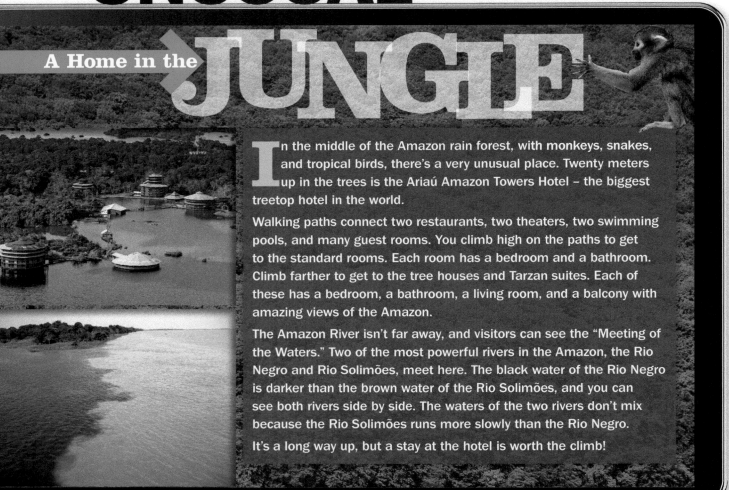

A Home in the JUNGLE

In the middle of the Amazon rain forest, with monkeys, snakes, and tropical birds, there's a very unusual place. Twenty meters up in the trees is the Ariaú Amazon Towers Hotel – the biggest treetop hotel in the world.

Walking paths connect two restaurants, two theaters, two swimming pools, and many guest rooms. You climb high on the paths to get to the standard rooms. Each room has a bedroom and a bathroom. Climb farther to get to the tree houses and Tarzan suites. Each of these has a bedroom, a bathroom, a living room, and a balcony with amazing views of the Amazon.

The Amazon River isn't far away, and visitors can see the "Meeting of the Waters." Two of the most powerful rivers in the Amazon, the Rio Negro and Rio Solimões, meet here. The black water of the Rio Negro is darker than the brown water of the Rio Solimões, and you can see both rivers side by side. The waters of the two rivers don't mix because the Rio Solimões runs more slowly than the Rio Negro.

It's a long way up, but a stay at the hotel is worth the climb!

Reading: An article about an unusual hotel

1. **Look at the photos. What do you see? Where do you think it is?**

 2. **Read and listen to the article. Why is the hotel unusual?**

3. **Read the article again. Answer the questions.**

   1. Which animals live near the hotel?

   _____

   2. How high up in the trees is the hotel?

   _____

   3. What rooms do tree houses and Tarzan suites have?

   _____

   4. What is the "Meeting of the Waters"?

   _____

4. **YOUR TURN** **Work with a partner. Would you like to stay in a treetop hotel? Why or why not?**

> I'd like to stay in a treetop hotel! I love nature and animals.

> I wouldn't like it because . . .

Grammar: Comparative and superlative adjectives and adverbs

5. Complete the chart.

Use comparative adjectives and adverbs to show how two things are different from each other.
Use superlative adjectives and adverbs to compare three or more things.

	Comparative		Superlative	
Adjectives	dark ➔ dark**er**	big ➔ _____	dark ➔ _____	big ➔ **the big**gest
	powerful ➔ **more**		popular ➔ _____	
	good ➔ **better**	bad ➔ **worse**	good ➔ **the best**	bad ➔ **the worst**
	The Rio Negro is _____ than the Rio Solimões.		The bathroom is **the darkest** room in the hotel.	
Adverbs	fast ➔ _____	slowly ➔ _____	fast ➔ **the fastest**	slowly ➔ **the most slowly**
	far ➔ far**ther**		far ➔ _____	
	well ➔ **better**	badly ➔ **worse**	well ➔ _____	badly ➔ **the worst**
	The Rio Solimões runs **more slowly than** the Rio Negro.		The water runs _____ in the summer.	

> Check your answers: Grammar reference, p. 111

6. Complete the sentences with the comparative adjectives or adverbs.

1. Brazil is ____*bigger than*____ (big) Mexico.

2. The Rio Negro runs _____ (fast) the Rio Solimões.

3. A vacation in the Amazon is _____ (exciting) a vacation in Antarctica.

4. The furniture in my room is _____ (good) the furniture in your room.

5. We got _____ (wet) our parents on the hike because they used umbrellas.

7. Circle the correct words.

In Spain, I toured the Guadix cave homes with my sister. They are some of the ¹**strangest / more strangely** homes in the world. People live in cave houses there. The houses are ²**more dark / darker** than normal houses because they don't have many windows.

In the summer, the caves are ³**cooler / coolest** than normal homes, and in winter they are ⁴**the warmer / warmer.**

Our tour guide spoke ⁵**quickest / more quickly** than most tour guides. He talked the ⁶**faster / fastest** near the end of the tour. My sister understood the guide ⁷**better / best** than I did, so she repeated everything ⁸**slower / more slowly** for me.

Speaking: Compare!

8. **YOUR TURN** **Discuss the questions with a partner.**

1. Who studies longer at night?

2. Who is better at sports?

> I study for an hour at night.

> I study for two hours. I study longer than you.

9. Join another pair. Compare your answers to Exercise 8. Then answer these questions.

1. Who studies the longest at night?

2. Who is the best at sports?

> Jack studies for four hours at night. He studies the longest.

BE CURIOUS — Find out about two people living in an old mine. What rooms are in the house? (Workbook, p. 82)

Discovery EDUCATION

6.1 A COOL LIFE

Things That PLUG IN

Listening: A clothing emergency

1. Who washes your clothes? Do you wash your own clothes?

2. Listen to Jackie tell her sister Chloe about her clothes. What's wrong with her pants? With her sweater?

3. Listen again and circle the correct answers.

   1. Jackie washed her dark and light clothes _____.

      a. together   b. separately   c. by hand

   2. Jackie's sweater is made of _____.

      a. cotton   b. jean material   c. wool

   3. Jackie washed her clothes on _____.

      a. hot   b. warm   c. cold

   4. Jackie learned how to fix her sweater from _____.

      a. her sister   b. a website   c. a label

Vocabulary: Household appliances

4. Write the words next to the correct numbers. Then listen and check your answers.

a dishwasher	a microwave	a toaster	an alarm clock
a hair dryer	a refrigerator	a vacuum cleaner	an iron
a lamp	✓ a stove	a washing machine	an oven

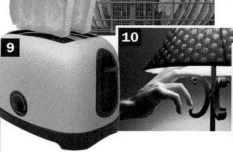

1. ___a stove___   5. _____   9. _____

2. _____   6. _____   10. _____

3. _____   7. _____   11. _____

4. _____   8. _____   12. _____

NOTICE IT
Fridge is short for *refrigerator*.

5. **YOUR TURN** Work with a partner. In what rooms do you use each of the household appliances in Exercise 4? How often do you use them?

> I use the stove in the kitchen. I use it two times a week.

Grammar: *should (not)*, *(not) have to*, *must (not)*

6. Complete the chart.

Use should not *for advice and recommendations.* Use have to *for responsibilities.*
Use not have to *for things that are not required.* Use must *for obligation.* Use must not *for prohibition.*

Affirmative	Negative
You _____ **wash** dark clothes separately. She **should look** at the labels.	You **shouldn't wash** darker clothes with lighter ones. She _____ **put** it in a sunny room.
You _____ **choose** the temperature first. It **has to be** cool.	You **don't have to wash** it by hand. It _____ **be** cold.
You **must use** cold water. They _____ **follow** the directions.	You _____ **use** hot water. They **must not miss** a step.

> Check your answers: Grammar reference, p. 111

7. Complete the sentences with the affirmative or negative of the words.

1. We ___*shouldn't put*___ (should / put) metal in the microwave. It can start a fire.

2. Sara _____ (have to / wash) her clothes today. She can do it tomorrow.

3. I _____ (should / get) a small hair dryer for my trip. My suitcase only has room for small things.

4. Jack and Paula _____ (have to / buy) a new dishwasher. Theirs broke.

5. Don _____ (must / use) his vacuum cleaner before 8:00 p.m. His parents don't like noise late at night.

8. Complete the sentences with *should (not)*, *(not) have to*, or *must (not)*.

1. Jenny _____ get a lamp for her bedroom. It's really dark.

2. The label says, "You _____ put the hair dryer in water." You will get hurt.

3. I _____ set my alarm clock on Saturday because I don't work on the weekend!

4. We _____ make the vegetables in the microwave. They're better on the stove.

5. My sister _____ wash her clothes at the laundromat. She doesn't have a washing machine at home.

> *Get it* **RIGHT!**
>
> Use **must** for obligation, not for things that are responsibilities.
> *You* **have to bring** *a pencil to class.*
> (= It's your responsibility to bring a pencil.)
> *You* **must use** *a pencil on the test.*
> (= It's an obligation to use a pencil. You're not allowed to use a pen or a marker.)

Speaking: Guess the appliance

9. **YOUR TURN** **Work with a partner. Think of an appliance. Describe it, and tell your partner how you *should (not)*, *(not) have to*, *must (not)* use it. Your partner guesses the appliance. Take turns.**

> It's small, and it's often white. You have to plug it in. You use it in the kitchen. You shouldn't put metal in it.

> Is it a microwave?

> Yes, it is!

At **Home**

Conversation: I have to clean the house.

1. **REAL TALK** Watch or listen to the teenagers. Are these reasons for preferring houses or apartments? Write *H* (house) or *A* (apartment).

   6.07

   1. ____ They're usually bigger.

   2. ____ They're quieter.

   3. ____ They usually have a garden.

   4. ____ They're usually closer to the center of a city.

2. **YOUR TURN** Which do *you* prefer – houses or apartments? Tell your partner. Give a reason for your answer.

3. Josh is helping Cara with her chores. Listen and complete the conversation.

   6.08

> **NOTICE IT**
> Some words are different in American English and British English.
>
> | American English | British English |
> |---|---|
> | *apartment* | *flat* |
> | *yard* | *garden* |

USEFUL LANGUAGE: Asking for and offering help

Can I ask you for a favor? | Could you help me out? | Would you like some help? | I'll give you a hand.

Josh: Are you ready to go the mall?

Cara: I'm sorry, but I can't go yet. I didn't finish my chores. I have to clean **the living room**.

Josh: ¹_____

Cara: Oh, yes. That'd be great. I'll **clean the furniture**, and you can **vacuum**.

Josh: OK. Let's get started.

Cara: I need to get the cleaning supplies out of that cabinet. I can't reach them.

Josh: Wait. ²_____

Cara: Great, thanks.

Josh: Hey . . . ³_____

Cara: Of course.

Josh: I need to get a birthday present for my sister. ⁴_____

Cara: Sure. Let's finish cleaning **the living room** and then shop for your sister.

4. Practice the conversation with a partner.

5. **YOUR TURN** Repeat the conversation in Exercise 3, but change the words in purple. Use the information in the chart for one conversation and your own ideas for another.

		Your ideas
Room to clean	the kitchen	
Chore #1	clean the sink	
Chore #2	put the dishes in the dishwasher	

To santiagoG@middleschool.cup.org
From jorge.vegasrg@net.cup.org
Subject My House

Hi Santiago,

I'm excited you're coming to stay with us in our new house for the summer! We live in a big house with four bedrooms. My parents have the biggest bedroom, and they have their own bathroom. My sister and I have our own bedrooms. There's a fourth bedroom, but now it's my mom's office. My bedroom is pretty big. I have two beds, so you can sleep in my room. There's room for your clothes in my dresser.

Downstairs there's a big living room. We have a sofa, two armchairs, and a huge TV! My favorite room is the kitchen. There's a big table where we eat, talk, and play games. There's a dishwasher, so we don't have to wash dishes by hand!

Tell me about your apartment.

Your cousin,

Jorge

Reading to write: A description of Jorge's house

6. **Look at the photo of Jorge's house. How many bedrooms do you think it has? Read the email to check.**

⊚ *Focus on* **CONTENT**
When you write about your house, include:
- the size, age, and kind of house
- how many bedrooms it has
- what other rooms it has
- your favorite room and why
- some of the furniture or appliances there

7. **Read Jorge's email again. What information does he include for each category from the Focus on Content box?**

⊚ *Focus on* **LANGUAGE**
Commas
Use commas to separate items in a list.
I have a desk, two chairs, and big bed in my bedroom.
Use commas to join two complete sentences with conjunctions like *and*, *but*, and *so*.
We usually cook in the oven, but sometimes we use the microwave.

8. **Find examples in Jorge's email of the comma rules in the Focus on Language box.**

9. **Put commas in the correct places.**

1. My bedroom is small but it's comfortable.

2. There are four chairs a big table and two lamps in our kitchen.

3. The dishwasher isn't working so I have to wash the dishes by hand.

4. I packed a hair dryer a toothbrush and shampoo in my suitcase.

Writing: An email about your house

◻ **PLAN**
Use the categories in the Focus on Content box and take notes about your home.

Size, age, and kind	
Number of bedrooms	
Other rooms	
Favorite room/why	
Furniture/appliances	

◻ **WRITE**
Write an email describing your house to a friend or someone in your family. Use your notes to help you. Write at least 80 words.

◻ **CHECK**
Check your writing. Can you answer "yes" to these questions?

• Is information for each category of the Focus on Content box in your description?

• Do you use commas correctly?

LIFE ON THE WATER

Did you know that some people live on the water? You can find houseboats on lakes, rivers, and canals all over the world. There are hundreds in Sausalito, California. Thirteen-year-old Ryan Harvey moved to a houseboat community with his family two years ago. We asked Ryan about a typical Saturday on his houseboat.

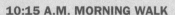

7:00 A.M. WILDLIFE WATCH
Early morning is the best time to see marine animals because it's the quietest time of the day. Sometimes, I can see seals right outside my bedroom window. They're amazing!

5:00 P.M. VISIT FRIENDS
We often go out in our kayaks to see other families on their boats. I paddle faster than my parents!

10:15 A.M. MORNING WALK
I go with Dad to get our mail at the marina. It's where all our neighbors meet. I always see my friends there.

7:00 P.M. DINNER
Dad makes dinner, and we eat on the balcony on top of our houseboat when the weather is nice. Because we're far from the town, there aren't any streetlights. You can see the stars at night!

1:00 P.M. LUNCH
The kitchen is very small, so only one person fits. Mom and I take turns making lunch. I usually cook more slowly than my mom.

"There's not much room on the houseboat, but you're closer to nature. It's also safer and quieter than the city. I love life on the water!"

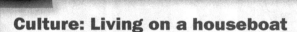

Culture: Living on a houseboat

1. **Look at the photos. Do you think the boy is at home or on vacation?**

2. **Read and listen to the article. What are some advantages to living on a houseboat? What are some disadvantages?**
   6.09

3. **Read the article again. Number the activities in order from 1–6.**
   - _3_ Ryan's mom cooks. → 3
   - _4_ Ryan's family eats outside. → 4
   - _1_ Ryan sees animals. — 1
   - _5_ Ryan's family goes out on the water. →5
   - ___ Ryan's dad cooks.
   - _2_ Ryan and his dad go for a walk. → 2

4. **YOUR TURN Work with a partner. Would you like to live on a houseboat? Why or why not? What other kind of house would you like to live in?**

   > I'd like to live on a houseboat because . . . I'd also like to live . . .

   > I wouldn't like to live on a houseboat because . . . I'd like to live . . .

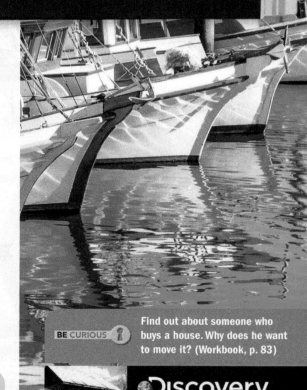

BE CURIOUS Find out about someone who buys a house. Why does he want to move it? (Workbook, p. 83)

Discovery EDUCATION

6.3 MOVING HOUSE

Vocabulary

1. Write the words for the furniture, items, and appliances next to the correct numbers.

1. Stufe
2. chair
3. Forn
4. FRidge
5. drawer
6. Vacuum Cleaver
7. bed
8. dRawers
9. MiRROR
10. desk
11. clock
12. Sofa

Grammar

2. Write sentences with the comparative or superlative form of the adjectives and adverbs.

1. these tablets / be / good / those laptops

   These tablets are very slowest.

   _____

2. Tara / have / comfortable / bed / in the house

   Tara has the most comfortable bed in the house.

3. we usually / walk / far / our cousins

   We usually walk very fast.

   _____

4. my dog / bark / loudly / your dog

   My dog is barckest dog.

   _____

5. the water / move / slowly / in the winter

   The water move the sand.

   _____

3. Circle the correct words.

1. Look at that sign. (You **must not**) / **don't have to** eat in the library.

2. You (**have to**) / **shouldn't** turn off the computer before you leave. It can't stay on all night.

3. You (**don't have to**) / **shouldn't** download any computer games onto the school computers. The teacher doesn't like it.

4. You (**should**) / **don't have to** cook tonight. I'm going to make dinner.

5. You (**must**) / **should** ask for help if you have a problem. It's a good idea.

Useful language

4. Look at the underlined words in the conversations. Write A if the person is asking for help. Write O if the person is offering help.

1. O

   A: The iron is up so high in that cabinet. I can't reach it.

   B: <u>Would you like some help?</u>

   A: Sure. That'd be great.

2. A

   A: I don't understand this recipe. <u>Could you help me out?</u>

   B: Sure. Let me see it.

3. A

   A: Hey, Sue. Do you want to go to a movie?

   B: Sure, but, <u>can I ask you for a favor</u> first?

   A: OK.

PROGRESS CHECK: Now I can . . .

☐ identify rooms in a house and household items.

☐ compare two or more rooms.

☐ identify and talk about household appliances.

☐ ask for and offer help.

☐ write an email about my house.

☐ talk about the kind of house I'd like to live in.

▶ **REVIEW UNITS 5–6, Workbook, pp. 42–43**

7 VISIONS *of the* FUTURE

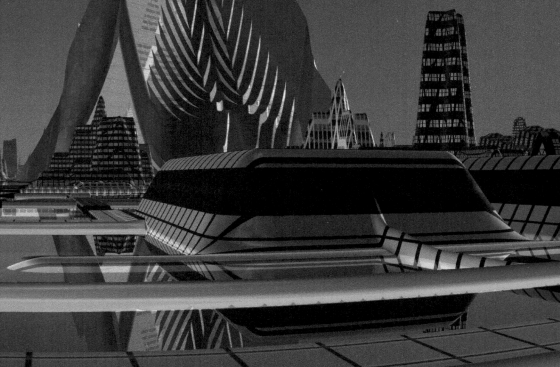

Discovery
EDUCATION™

BE CURIOUS

▶ A Pizza Robot

▶ How important is your cell phone?

▶ Music Sharing

▶ The Secret of the Pyramids

1. What is this city like? How is it different from our cities today?

2. How do you think people communicate in this city?

3. Would you like to live in a place like this? Why or why not?

UNIT CONTENTS

Vocabulary Computers and communication; technology verbs

Grammar *Will* and *won't* for predictions; adverbs of possibility; first conditional with *will* (*not*), *may* (*not*), and *might* (*not*)

Listening They're always coming out with something new.

Vocabulary: Computers and communication

1. Match the words (a–i) with the correct pictures.

a. a keyboard   d. a printer   g. a touch pad

b. a flash drive   e. a smartphone   h. a touch screen

c. a mouse   f. a tablet   ✓ i. Wi-Fi

1. [i]   2. [ ]   3. [ ]   4. [ ]

5. [ ] 6. [ ]   7. [ ]   8. [ ]   9. [ ]

2. Listen, check, and repeat. 🔊 7.01

3. Circle the correct words.

1. Do you usually use **Wi-Fi / (a touch pad)** or a mouse?

2. You can save your work on **a flash drive / a touch pad.**

3. You use **Wi-Fi / a printer** to go on the Internet.

4. You use **a mouse / a keyboard** to type an email.

5. You can carry **a smartphone / a touch screen** easily in one hand.

6. I prefer **a flash drive / a mouse** to a touch pad.

🔊 7.02 ➡️ *Say it* **RIGHT!**

The letters **ou** can sound like the /uh/ or /ow/ sound. Listen to the sentence.
My cousin has three computers in her house.
Which words in Exercise 1 have the letters **ou**? What sounds do they make?

Speaking: A computer quiz

4. YOUR TURN Use the words from Exercise 1 to give information about you.

Something I use:

• at school: _____

• to do homework: _____

• at home: _____

• every day: _____

• to play games: _____

• to communicate with friends: _____

5. Work with a partner. Share your answers to the quiz in Exercise 4.

I use Wi-Fi, a printer, and a touch pad at school.

▶ Workbook, p. 44

Reading Computers: A Big Past, A Small Future; How do you think people will listen to music in the future?; Television Grows Up . . . and Down!

Conversation Asking for and giving instructions

Writing An opinion paragraph

The Future of Technology

Computers: A Big Past, A Small Future

Over 65 years ago, the world's first computer was "born." Scientists called it "The Baby," but it was huge. It filled an entire room! Three people made the computer and programmed math problems for it. On June 19, 1948, the computer solved its first math problem – in 52 minutes! At that time, this was amazing.

Computers are now much smaller. With touch-screen technology, many computers don't need extra things, like a keyboard or a mouse. In the future, computers probably won't need these things at all. Some computers, like the smartphone, can fit in one hand. Computers are also more powerful today. There is more computing power in a smartphone than there was in all of the computers on *Apollo 11*, the first spacecraft to take people to the moon!

How else will computers change in the future? A computer's "brain" is a chip inside the computer, and in the future, people will definitely be able to save much more information on a computer chip. So, computers will be smaller and even more powerful. Perhaps they'll even think like humans! Maybe we won't need to tell computers what to do because they'll decide for themselves!

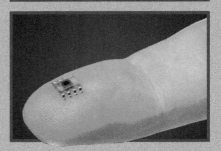

Reading: An article about computers

1. **Work with a partner. Look at the photo of an old computer. How was it different from modern computers?**

 2. **Read and listen to the article. What was the first computer like?**

3. **Read the article again. Circle the correct answers.**

   1. The first computer fit in _____.

      a. a hand   b. a room   (c. a building)

   2. The Baby found the answer to _____ math problem(s) in 52 minutes.

      (a. 1)   b. 3   c. 65

   3. The computers on *Apollo 11* were _____ a smartphone.

      (a. more powerful than)   b. less powerful than   c. as powerful as

   4. Today, many computers don't have _____.

      (a. keyboards)   b. chips   c. touch screens

4. **YOUR TURN** **Work with a partner. Think of at least five things you think computers should do in the future.**

   > Computers should clean our houses in the future. They should . . .

5. **YOUR TURN** **Join another pair. Share your ideas from Exercise 4. Which idea do you think is the best?**

DID YOU KNOW...?

There are more than two billion personal computers in the world today, including tablets and smartphones.

Grammar: *will* and *won't* for predictions

6. Complete the chart.

Use will and won't to predict future events.

Wh- questions	Affirmative answers	Negative answers	
What **will** my smartphone **do** in the future?	Perhaps it'**ll think** like a human.	It _____ **drive** a car.	
How _____ computers **change**?	They _____ **be** smaller.	They **won't be** bigger.	
Yes/No questions	Short answers		
_____ my smartphone **think** like a human?	Yes, it **will**.	No, it _____.	
Will computers **change**?	Yes, they _____.	No, they **won't**.	
Contractions: I will = I'**ll** you will = you'**ll** he will = he'**ll** she will = she'**ll** it will = _____ we will = we'**ll** they will = _____			

> Check your answers: Grammar reference, p. 112

7. In 1900, an American engineer made these predictions. Complete them with *will* or *won't* and the correct verbs.

> buy   eat   not be   not cook   ✓not live   not wait   talk

1. Animals ___*won't live*___ in the wild.
2. People _____ on wireless phones.
3. We _____ all of our own meals. We _____ them in stores.
4. The letters *C*, *X*, and *Q* _____ in the alphabet.
5. We _____ until summer to eat vegetables. We _____ them in winter.

8. Work with a partner. Which predictions in Exercise 7 are true now?

9. Write sentences about the future with *will* and *won't*. How sure are you? Use *definitely, certainly, probably, maybe,* or *perhaps*.

1. we / have / Wi-Fi connections in our clothes

   We'll probably have Wi-Fi connections in our clothes.

2. cars / not need / human drivers

   _____

3. people / live / to be 120 years old

   _____

4. we / not use / pens and pencils

   _____

Adverbs of possibility

Sure	Pretty sure	Not as sure
definitely certainly	probably	maybe perhaps

Use adverbs of possibility to say how sure you are about a prediction. **Definitely**, **certainly**, and **probably** come between the subject and **will** or **won't**, or between **will** and the base form of the verb. **Perhaps** and **maybe** come before the subject.

They **definitely** will think like humans.

They'll **probably** think like humans.

Perhaps they will think like humans.

Speaking: Predictions about my future

10. YOUR TURN Work with a partner. Ask and answer questions about the future. Make predictions about the items below or your own ideas.

> your school/job   your friends/family   your town/city   your computer

> What will you do in the future?

> I'll probably write software for computers.

BE CURIOUS

Find out about a new technology. How do the people get pizza? (Workbook, p. 84)

Discovery EDUCATION

7.1 A PIZZA ROBOT

Using
TECHNOLOGY

Listening: They're always coming out with something new.

1. Do you and your friends play video games? What do you play?

7.04 2. Listen to Jenna and Karl talk about a video game. Who wants to work with computers in the future?

7.04 3. Listen again. Are the sentences true (*T*) or false (*F*)?

1. Karl has a new game console. ___

2. There aren't any boy characters in Cyber Chase. ___

3. Jenna and Karl play Ocean World. ___

4. Jenna wants a game console for her birthday. ___

5. Karl thinks Jenna should get a Ztron 2100. ___

6. Karl is taking a computer class. ___

Vocabulary: Technology verbs

7.05 4. Match the pictures with the correct sentences. Then listen and check your answers.

1. _c_ To see the bottom of the web page, **scroll down**. To go back to the top, **scroll up**.

2. ___ **Click on** the item you want.

3. ___ To see more of the city on the map, **zoom out**. To look at your street, **zoom in**.

4. ___ You can **sign into** your web page from any computer. Don't forget to **sign out** when you're done!

5. ___ Do you **shut down** your computer at night?

6. ___ **Turn on** your computer with the power button.

7. ___ I **back up** my files every day.

5. **YOUR TURN** Work with a partner. Tell your partner how to do one of these things on a computer. Use the phrases in Exercise 4.

| listen to music | read a blog | watch a video | write an email |

> Turn on your computer. Then sign into your email account. Next, . . .

Grammar: First conditional with *will* (*not*), *may* (*not*), and *might* (*not*)

6. Complete the chart.

> Use the first conditional to show results or possible results of future actions. Use *if* and the simple present in the main clause and *will* (*not*), *may* (*not*), or *might* (*not*) and the base form of a verb in the result clause.

Statements

You**'ll see** all of the choices **if** you **zoom out**.

If I **make** games, they **won't be** boring.

_____I F_____ I **ask** my parents, they **might get** it for me for my birthday.

I **may not get** the Ztron 2100 _____I F_____ a newer model **comes** out.

Questions

What kind of games _____will_____ you **make if** you**'re** a designer?   Action games.

If I **beat** you, **will** you **do** my homework?   Yes, I **will**. / No, I _____won't_____.

> Check your answers: Grammar reference, p. 112

Check your answers: Grammar reference, p. 112

NOTICE IT

The *if* clause can come at the beginning or end of the sentence. Use a comma after the *if* clause when it comes at the beginning.
If you scroll down, you'll see more characters.
You'll see more characters if you scroll down.

7. Circle the correct words.

1. If Joe **learns** / **might learn** to write code, he **gets** / **might get** a great tech job.

2. If my parents **get** / **will get** a new computer, they **don't buy** / **won't buy** a tablet.

3. You **don't lose** / **won't lose** your files if you **back** / **may back** them up.

4. I **buy** / **may buy** a new smartphone if I **get** / **will get** enough money for my birthday.

5. **Will I get** / **Do I get** to your blog if I **click on** / **will click on** this link?

6. If my computer **stops** / **will stop** working, I **don't finish** / **may not finish** my homework.

7. If you **decide** / **will decide** to get a printer, which one **do you buy** / **will you buy?**

8. Your tablet **shuts down** / **will shut down** if you **click on** / **will click on** that.

Get it RIGHT!

Do not use the simple present in the main clause with the first conditional.
I'll win if we play that game.
NOT: ~~I win if we play that game.~~

8. Complete the paragraph with the simple present or *will* (*not*).

If I [1] _____pass_____ (pass) all of my exams, my parents [2] _____will buy_____ (buy) me a new tablet. If I [3] _____get_____ (get) a new tablet, I [4] _____will start_____ (start) my own website. I [5] _____will post_____ (post) a video of my dog riding a skateboard if I [6] _____makes_____ (make) my own website. If one million people [7] _____like_____ (like) my video, I [8] _____will be_____ (be) famous! I [9] _____won't be_____ (not be) famous if no one [10] _____watch_____ (watch) my video. If I [11] _____fail_____ (fail) any of my exams, my parents [12] _____won't buy_____ (not buy) me a tablet. I should start studying!

Speaking: A lot of *Ifs*!

9. **YOUR TURN** **Ask and answer questions with the ideas below or your own ideas. Use *will* (*not*), *may* (*not*), or *might* (*not*).**

> If I have a website in the future, . . .   If I buy a computer in the future, . . .
> If I make a video in the future, . . .

> What will you post if you have a website in the future?

> If I have a website, I'll post funny videos.

Tech
TRENDS

Conversation: Using your cell phone

7.06

1. **REAL TALK** Watch or listen to the teenagers. How many think their cell phones are important? How many don't think they're important? Write the numbers.

Important	Not important
12456	3

2. **YOUR TURN** How important is *your* cell phone? Tell your partner.

7.07

3. Kendra is telling her grandmother how to make a call on a smartphone. Listen and complete the conversation.

USEFUL LANGUAGE: Asking for and giving instructions

you need to	all you have to	how do I	How does it work?

Grandma: Can I borrow your phone to **call Grandpa**?

Kendra: Sure. Here's my smartphone.

Grandma: ¹____How does it work?____ ✓

Kendra: First, ²____You need to____ press the round button to turn it on. ✓

Grandma: Like this?

Kendra: Yes. That's it. See . . . it's a touch screen. Now, click on the **phone** icon.

Grandma: OK. So, ³____how do I____ make a call? ✓

Kendra: **Click on the contacts icon and scroll down to Grandpa's name.**

Grandma: OK. Now what?

Kendra: ⁴____all you have to____ do is **click on his name**. ✓

Grandma: I see. That was easy!

4. Practice the conversation with a partner.

5. **YOUR TURN** Repeat the conversation in Exercise 3, but change the words in purple. Use the information in the chart for one conversation and your own ideas for another.

		My ideas
Task	text Aunt Linda	
Type of icon	text message	
Task	send a text	
Step 1	scroll down to Aunt Linda's name and click on it	
Step 2	type your text and click on "send"	

TechIt Question of the Week:

How do you think people will listen to music in the future?   Marcus Howard   posted 10/18

In my opinion, people will listen to music from computer chips in their clothing. One reason is that it will be an easy way to listen to music. People won't need to carry MP3 players or even smartphones for music. Small computer chips will be in sunglasses, hats, jackets, and shirts. Another reason is that some of this technology exists already. For example, you can buy sunglasses that play music. If this trend continues, it will be popular in the future. In conclusion, I think people will listen to music in their clothing, and it will be great!

👍 2   👎 0

Reading to write: An opinion paragraph

6. Look at the title and the photo. How does Marcus think people will listen to music in the future? Read his paragraph to check.

⊚ *Focus on* **CONTENT**
In an opinion paragraph, include:
- **A** an introduction to the topic and your opinion
- **B** reasons for your opinion
- **C** facts and examples to support your reasons
- **D** a conclusion with your opinion

7. Read Marcus's paragraph again. Label the sentences in the paragraph with the items in the Focus on Content box (A–D).

⊚ *Focus on* **LANGUAGE**
You can use these phrases in opinion pieces:
To give opinions: ***In my opinion,***   ***I think (that)***
                          I believe (that)
To give reasons: ***One reason***   ***Another reason***
                          is (that)   ***is (that)***
To conclude: ***In conclusion,***   ***For these reasons,***

8. Find examples of the phrases in the Focus on Language box in Marcus's paragraph.

9. Complete the paragraph.

| another reason is that | I believe that | one reason is that |
| for these reasons | in my opinion | |

[1]_____, people will ride in cars without drivers in the future. [2]_____ it will make streets safer. The cars will drive themselves with new technology. If people don't drive, accidents won't happen. [3]_____ it will save people a lot of money. The cars will be electric, and people won't have to buy gas. [4]_____ this will happen because the technology already exists. [5]_____, people won't drive cars in the future.

Writing: Your opinion paragraph

◻ **PLAN**
Choose one of the topics about the future or your own idea. Write notes about it.

How do you think people will . . . in the future?

communicate with each other	listen to music
read books	shop
travel	use their smartphones

Topic and opinion: _____

Reason	Fact / Example

◻ **WRITE**
Write an opinion paragraph about your topic. Use your notes to help you. Write at least 80 words.

◻ **CHECK**
Check your writing. Can you answer "yes" to these questions?

- Is information for each category from the Focus on Content box in your paragraph?

- Do you use the expressions from the Focus on Language box correctly?

Television Grows Up . . . and Down!

People in every country and every culture watch television. You watch TV differently than your parents and grandparents did. And TV watching will probably be different in the future.

The story of TV started over 80 years ago. In 1936, there were only about 200 televisions. Sixty years later, there were one billion TVs worldwide. The first TVs were big, square boxes, and the TV shows were in black and white. People had to get off the couch to turn on the TV and change the channel with a button on the front of the TV. Color TVs arrived in the 1950s. Today, all TVs are in color, and people change the channel with remote controls. And there are more channels. When TV started, there were only a few channels, and now there are hundreds!

In 1973, the first big-screen TV was in stores. Today, TVs are getting bigger – and smaller. People have huge flat-screen TVs, and some have surround sound. It's like being at a movie theater at home. "TVs" are also getting smaller. Many people watch TV shows on their tablets and smartphones. Some shows are only available online.

How will people watch TV in the future? Some newer inventions are 3D television and smart TVs with Wi-Fi connections. Some people say our TVs at home will get even bigger, while the gadgets we watch TV on will get smaller; for example, there are "TV watches" and "TV glasses." Most people agree that TV watching will definitely stay popular.

Culture: How we watch TV

1. Look at the photos. How are TVs today different than they were in the past?

2. Read and listen to the article. What is the main idea?

a. how we watch TV today

b. the history of TV watching

c. the future of TV watching

3. Read the article again. Are the sentences true or false? Write _T_ (true), _F_ (false), or _NI_ (no information).

1. The first TVs were in color and black and white. F

2. In 1996, there were about one billion TVs in the world. NI

3. Today, there are over 500 TV channels. T

4. Big TVs aren't popular today because people watch shows on their phones. F

5. There are some shows you can only watch online. T

6. In the future, everyone will watch 3D TV shows. T

4. YOUR TURN Work with a partner. How do you watch TV now? How do you think you'll watch TV in the future?

Workbook, p. 85

DID YOU KNOW . . . ?
The remote control arrived in 1956. Surround sound, sound that comes from speakers instead of just the TV, was first available for TVs in 1982.

BE CURIOUS — Find out about Napster. What is it? (Workbook, p. 85)

Discovery
EDUCATION

7.3 MUSIC SHARING

Vocabulary

1. Label the photos with the correct words.

1. ___Mouse___   3. ___Keyboard___

2. ___Printer___   4. ___UsB___

2. Circle the correct words.

1. How often do you **scroll up** / (**back up**) your files?

2. If you (**zoom in**) / **sign into**, you can see my house on the map.

3. Will you please **turn on** / (**shut down**) my computer when you're done with it?

4. (**Click on**) / **Zoom out** that link to see the photos I posted.

Grammar

3. Write sentences about the future with *will* or *won't* and the word in parentheses.

1. Everyone works at home. (probably)

   Everyone will probably work at home.

2. People have robots in their houses. (perhaps)

   People perhaps have Robots ...

3. Students don't use flash drives. (definitely)

   students definitely don't use ...

4. We go to the moon for vacation. (maybe)

   Maybe we go to the moon ...

4. Match the phrases to make sentences.

1. If you're going to be late, _d_
2. If you get a smaller computer, _A_
3. If I don't study tonight, _b_
4. What will you do _C_

a. if your computer breaks?

b. I won't pass my test tomorrow.

c. will you send me a text message?

d. it will be easier to carry.

Useful language

5. Circle the correct answers.

1. **A:** This is a great new video game.

   B: How does it (**work**) / **need** / **do**?

2. **A:** **What** / **How** / (**Who**) do I send an email from my phone?

   B: First, sign into your email account.

3. **A:** Can you help me download this app?

   B: Sure. First, you **need to** / (**click on**) / **will to** go to the app store.

4. **A:** How do I shut down my tablet?

   B: All you **like to** / **don't have to** / (**have to**) do is hold that button down for a few seconds.

PROGRESS CHECK: Now I can . . .

☐ talk about computers and technology.	☐ ask for and give instructions.
☐ make predictions about the future.	☐ write an opinion paragraph.
☐ talk about how to use technology.	☐ talk about how I watch TV today and in the future.

CLIL PROJECT

7.4 The Secret of the Pyramids, p. 119

8 The CHOICES We MAKE

BE CURIOUS

A School at Home

What are you going to do when you leave school?

Time for an Adventure!

1. What decision do you think this person has to make?

2. What decisions do you have to make in your life?

3. What do you do when you have to make a difficult decision?

UNIT CONTENTS

Vocabulary Life events; containers and materials
Grammar *be going to* and *will*; present continuous and simple present for future
Listening An eco-project

Vocabulary: Life events

1. Match the pictures (a–j) with the correct words and phrases.

1. _h_ be born
2. ___ finish school
3. ___ get a job
4. ___ get married
5. ___ get your driver's license
6. ___ go to college
7. ___ go to school
8. ___ have children
9. ___ retire
10. ___ take a year off

2. Listen, check, and repeat.

3. In which order do people usually do the life events in Exercise 1?

> First, people are born. Then they go to school. After that . . .

Speaking: About someone's life

4. YOUR TURN Work with a partner. Tell your partner about a parent's life or the life of another relative or adult you know. What do they have in common?

> My mother was born in 1967. She went to school in Durango, Mexico. She went to college at the University of Texas. After college, she got a job at . . .

> My Uncle Jim was born in 1967, too. But he went to school in . . .

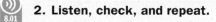
Workbook, p. 50

Reading Life in the Outback; Farah's Application Letter; A Summer in Alaska
Conversation Agreeing and disagreeing
Writing An application letter

UNUSUAL LIVES
Life in the Outback

by Lauren Birch
The outback is a large area in the middle of Australia. Not many people live there, and most of them are sheep farmers. Matt Clark lives on a "sheep station" with his parents and sister. I interviewed Matt to find out about life in the outback.

Q **Do you work?**

A Yes. I help my parents on the farm and take care of the sheep. It's very hard, but I love it!

Q **Where do you go to school?**

A My sister and I go to the "school of the air." We have classes with other kids and a teacher on our computer. We can see and hear each other with web cams. We take quizzes and tests online, and we also email homework to our teacher.

Q **How do you see friends?**

A My friends live far away, but we're lucky because my family has a small airplane. We fly to the nearest town every month to see friends and go shopping. My school has special events, too. I'm going to go to a camp next month!

Q **What are you going to do after you finish school? Will you stay on the farm?**

A I'm going to study agriculture in college in Sydney. But I think I'll come back here to live. I was born here, and this is my home.

DID YOU KNOW...?
About 60,000 people live in the outback, and there are over 70 million sheep!

Reading: An interview about life in the outback

1. **Look at the photos. Where do you think it is? Would you want to live there?**

 2. **Read and listen to the article. Why does the reporter interview Matt?**

   a. to find out about an unusual school

   b. to find out about life on a sheep farm

   c. to find out about his college plans

3. **Read the article again. Are the sentences true (*T*) or false (*F*)? Correct the false sentences.**

   1. Most Australians live in the center of Australia. ___

   2. Matt works with his parents. ___

   3. Matt flies in a plane to get to school. ___

   4. Matt's friends don't live near his sheep station. ___

   5. Matt's family goes to a town every week. ___

   6. Matt plans to leave his home and return in the future. ___

4. **YOUR TURN Work with a partner. Answer the questions.**

   1. How is Matt's life different from your life?

   > Matt's life is different from mine because he has to work, and . . .

   2. What do you think are the positive and negative things about life in the outback?

   > One positive thing is . . .

Grammar: *be going to* and *will*

5. Complete the chart.

Use be going to *to talk about plans in the future.*
Use will *to talk about predictions and unplanned decisions.*

be going to	will
Wh- questions and answers	
What **are** you **going to do**?	Where **will** he **live**?
I'm _____ study agriculture.	He**'ll live** in the outback.
I'm **not going to study** history.	He _____ **live** in Sydney.
Yes/No questions and answers	
Is he **going to study** history?	_____ you **stay** here?
Yes, he _____. / No, he **isn't**.	Yes, I **will**. / No, I **won't**.

> Check your answers: Grammar reference, p. 113

Say it RIGHT!

The *i* in **will** is a short **I** (/ɪ/), and the *e* in **we'll** is a long **e** (/e/). However, in speaking, **will** and **we'll** often sound alike. They both can sound like /wɪl/. Listen to the sentences.
I will get married to Tom next year.
We'll get married in May.
Ask and answer the questions in Exercise 6 with a partner. Pay attention to the pronunciation of **will** and **we'll**.

6. Match the questions with the answers.

1. _e_ Will Sheila retire next year?
2. ___ When are you going to go to college?
3. ___ Will you get your driver's licenses in June?
4. ___ Are Tom and Rita getting married next month?
5. ___ When will you finish school?
6. ___ Is Lily going to have children?

a. No, they're not.
b. Yes, she is.
c. I'm going to start in September.
d. We'll be done in a year.
e. Yes, she will.
f. No, we won't. We'll get them in July.

7. Complete the conversation with the correct form of *be going to* for future plans or *will* for predictions and unplanned decisions.

Mom: I'm worried about Neil.

Dad: Why? What's the problem?

Mom: He says he ¹ *is going to get* (get) an after-school job.

Dad: That ² _____ (be) really difficult! ³ _____ he _____ (stop) playing soccer?

Mom: No, he ⁴ _____ (stay) on the team.

Dad: When ⁵ _____ he _____ (study)?

Mom: I don't know. I don't think he should get a job until the summer.

Dad: I agree! Maybe he ⁶ _____ (change) his mind. I ⁷ _____ (talk) to him tonight.

Mom: You can try, but he probably ⁸ _____ (not listen) to you.

NOTICE IT
Think, *probably*, and *maybe* are often used with *will* for predictions and unplanned events.
He *thinks* he*'ll live* in the outback.
He *probably won't live* in Sydney.
Maybe they*'ll get* married next year.

Speaking: Future plans and predictions

8. **YOUR TURN** Work with a partner. First, tell your partner about what you are going to do or not going to do in the future. Then give predictions about what you will or won't do.

> I'm going to take a year off when I finish school. I'm not going to start college right away. I think I'll go to Brazil. I'll probably go to the rain forest. I don't think I'll go to Rio . . . .

Find out about children who are homeschooled. What are some subjects they study? (Workbook, p. 86)

8.1 A SCHOOL AT HOME

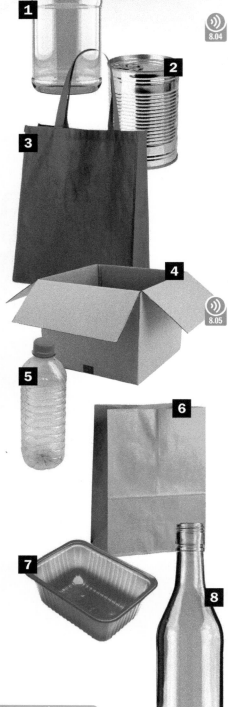

Cleaning UP

Listening: An eco-project

1. **Do you know anyone who took a year off after finishing high school? What did he or she do?**

2. **Listen to Olivia tell Dan about her sister's plans for a year off. What are her sister's plans?**

3. **Listen again. Circle the correct answers.**

   1. Olivia's sister is going to _____.
      - a. Costa Rica
      - b. Europe

   2. She's going to _____.
      - a. help sea turtles
      - b. pick up trash

   3. She'll probably work in _____.
      - a. a surf shop
      - b. a restaurant

   4. Olivia wants to _____ after she finishes high school.
      - a. travel in Europe
      - b. work in Paris

   5. Dan wants to work _____ before he goes to college.
      - a. on an eco-project
      - b. at home

Vocabulary: Containers and materials

4. **Look at the pictures. Write the phrases next to the correct numbers. Then listen and check your answers.**

a cardboard box	a glass bottle	a metal can	a plastic bottle
a cloth bag	✓ a glass jar	a paper bag	a plastic carton

1. _____a glass jar_____   5. _____
2. ___cloth bag___   6. ___paper bag___
3. ___metal can___   7. ___plastic carton___
4. ___cardboard box___   8. ___glass bottle___

5. **Work with a partner. Answer the questions.**

   1. What things come in the containers in Exercise 4?

   > Peanut butter comes in a glass jar or a plastic jar.

   > Pasta sauce does, too.

   2. Do you recycle containers in your home? What do you recycle?

   > In my home, we recycle . . .

Grammar: Present continuous and simple present for future

6. Complete the chart.

As with *be going to*, use the present continuous to talk about future plans. Use the simple present to talk about scheduled future events.

Present continuous	Simple present
Wh- questions and answers	
Why _____ she **going** there?	When _____ she **start** the project?
She**'s taking** a year off.	She **starts** next week.
She**'s not traveling**.	She **doesn't start** tomorrow.
Yes/No questions and answers	
_____ they **helping** the turtles?	**Does** class **start** in five minutes?
Yes, they **are**. / No, they _____.	Yes, it _____. / No, it **doesn't**.

> Check your answers: Grammar reference, p. 113

7. Complete the sentences with the present continuous or simple present.

I ¹ _'m going_ (go) to a class at the recycling center next week. The class ² _____ (be) on Tuesday. It ³ _____ (start) at 10:00 a.m., and it ⁴ _____ (end) at 4:00 p.m. My friend Vic ⁵ _____ (take) the class with me. We ⁶ _____ (not drive) to the recycling center. We ⁷ _____ (walk). Two people ⁸ _____ (teach) how to make chairs out of recycled cardboard boxes. I ⁹ _____ (not collect) boxes for the class because the recycling center ¹⁰ _____ (provide) the boxes next week.

Get it **RIGHT!**

Use the present continuous, not *will*, to talk about future arrangements.
I'm going to Italy on July 15.
NOT: ~~I'll go to Italy on July 15.~~

8. Correct the mistakes in the underlined words.

1. My roommate and I <u>recycle</u> our metal cans tomorrow.

2. The class <u>started</u> at 8:00 a.m. tomorrow.

3. I'm excited because I<u>'ll volunteer</u> at a recycling center next month.

4. We <u>are having</u> a meeting for the eco-project at 11:00 next Tuesday.

5. My sister and I <u>will go</u> to Costa Rica on May 10.

Speaking: Reuse it!

9. YOUR TURN Choose a container from the Vocabulary on page 78, and think of something you can make out of it. Then plan a class to teach people how to make the object. Fill out the chart.

Type of container	
What you will make	
Date of the class	
Where the class is	
When the class will start	
When the class will end	

10. Work with a partner. Tell your partner about your class. Your partner asks questions.

In my class, I'm teaching people how to make flower vases out of plastic bottles.

How many vases are you making?

MARINE BIOLOGY

Our FUTURES

Conversation: I'm going to get a degree.

1. **REAL TALK** Watch or listen to the teenagers. Check (✓) the things they are going to do when they leave school.

- ☐ be the leader of a country
- ☐ buy something
- ☐ get a driver's license
- ☐ have children
- ☐ marry someone
- ☐ play a sport
- ☐ study a language
- ☐ visit someone
- ☐ volunteer somewhere
- ☐ work

2. **YOUR TURN** What are *you* going to do when you leave school? Tell your partner.

3. Listen to Lenny and Katie talking about their plans for when they finish school. Complete the conversation.

USEFUL LANGUAGE: Agreeing and disagreeing

| Absolutely! | I disagree | I suppose you're right. | Maybe, but I think |

Katie: I can't believe we'll finish school **in two years**! What are you going to do then?

Lenny: I'm definitely going to college.

Katie: What are you going to study?

Lenny: I think I'll study **marine biology**!

Katie: Wow! That's going to be difficult.

Lenny: ¹_____ I'll love the **science** classes, so it won't be too hard. What about you?

Katie: I'm going to take a year off. I want to volunteer at **a recycling center**. I think it's important.

Lenny: ²_____ Not enough people care about helping **the environment**.

Katie: Well, ³_____. A lot of people do things to help **the environment**.

Lenny: ⁴_____

4. Practice the conversation with a partner.

5. **YOUR TURN** Repeat the conversation in Exercise 3, but change the words in purple. Use the information in the chart for one conversation and your own ideas for another.

		Your ideas
Finish school	in May	
Subject to study	engineering	
Type of classes	math	
Where to volunteer	an animal shelter	
Who/What to help	animals	

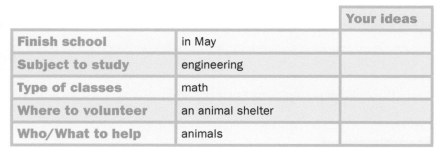

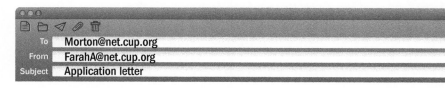

To: Morton@net.cup.org
From: FarahA@net.cup.org
Subject: Application letter

Dear Mr. Morton:

I am interested in volunteering at Clinton Hospital this summer. One day, I want to be a doctor and get a job in a hospital. I'm going to college in the fall, and I'm going to study medicine.

I'd like to help sick people. My mother was sick last year, and she had wonderful doctors. This inspired me to become a doctor. I want to help people have healthier lives.

For these reasons, I'd like to volunteer at your hospital. I'd work in any area, but I'd rather work with patients. Thank you for considering me for this volunteer position.

Sincerely,

Farah Ajam

Reading to write: An application letter

6. **Look at the photo of Farah. What kind of job do you think she wants in the future? Read the email to check.**

 Focus on **CONTENT**
When you write an application letter, include this information:
- **1** The position you're interested in
- **2** Your long-term goals
- **3** Your motivation for wanting the position
- **4** Repeat the position you're interested in
- **5** Thank the person you're writing to

7. **Read Farah's letter again. What information does she include for each step in the Focus on Content box? Write the numbers by the sentences.**

 Focus on **LANGUAGE**
want, would like ('d like), would rather ('d rather)
Use the infinitive form of a verb after **want** and **would like** to talk about things you want in the future.
 - *He **wants to be** a scientist. He**'d like to work** with animals.*
Use the base form of a verb after **would rather** to talk about a preference.
 - *I don't want to work in a hospital. **I'd rather work** in a doctor's office.*
 - *I**'d rather work** in a doctor's office **than** in a hospital.*

8. **Find examples in Farah's letter of the expressions in the Focus on Language box.**

9. **Complete the sentences with the infinitive or base form of the verbs.**

   1. Dina and Marcos want _____ (get) married in the spring.

   2. I'd rather _____ (use) these cardboard boxes than throw them away.

   3. Jenny would like _____ (retire) at age 60.

   4. We don't want _____ (go) to college right away. We'd rather _____ (take) a year off first.

   5. I'd like _____ (help) people learn about recycling.

 Writing: Your application letter

○ **PLAN**
First, think about a volunteer position that interests you. Choose one of these volunteer opportunities or use your own idea. Take notes.

a day-care center	a park
a library	a sea turtle program
a recycling center	

The position: _____

Your long-term goals	Your motivation
_____	_____
_____	_____
_____	_____

○ **WRITE**
Write an application letter for the volunteer opportunity. Use your notes to help you. Write at least 80 words.

○ **CHECK**
Check your writing. Can you answer "yes" to these questions?

- Is information for each category from the Focus on Content box in your letter?

- Do you use *want, would like,* and *would rather* correctly?

Workbook, pp. 54–55

A SUMMER IN ALASKA

Do you have summer plans? Are you looking for an interesting experience? Then do something different and discover Alaska. We organize summer activities for young people. Help others and gain experience in a possible future career! Here are our three most popular programs.

A MARINE VOLUNTEER

Work with professional ocean scientists at an aquarium and wildlife rescue center. You'll learn about octopuses, sea lions, and other ocean animals. You'll learn from the scientists as they study these animals. Volunteers help with research and animal rescue, and they teach others about marine life. This is a great first step to a career in marine biology!

B PARK VOLUNTEER

Work in one of the many parks in Alaska. You'll stay in a cabin right in the park and use public showers and a dining room near your cabin. You'll help keep the park clean, and you'll learn a lot about Alaska's wild animals, like bears and moose. Many volunteers will take park visitors on hikes and tell them about Alaska's plants and animals. This is an excellent experience for people interested in a job in conservation.

C COMMUNITY VOLUNTEER

Work and live in a local Alaskan community. You can work at a school and help children with their schoolwork and teach them computer skills. You'll even have the chance to start your own program. For example, you could start a recycling program or an afterschool club. You'll teach others, and you'll also learn about life in the community. It is a good experience for people interested in a teaching career.

Culture: Volunteer programs in Alaska

1. Look at the photos of volunteer activities in Alaska. What do you see? What do you think the volunteers do for each job?

2. Read and listen to the article. Match the volunteer programs in the article (A–C) with the future careers (1–3).

   1. a conservationist ___

   2. a teacher ___

   3. a marine biologist ___

3. Read the article again. Answer the questions.

   1. Who are the volunteer projects for? _____

   2. Where do park volunteers live? _____

   3. In which program can you start your own project?

      _____

   4. Which programs involve animals? _____

   5. Which programs involve teaching others? _____

4. **YOUR TURN** Work with a partner. Which place would you like to volunteer? Why? Do you know of any similar projects in your city or country?

   > I'd like to volunteer at a park because I love nature.

   > In my country, there's a . . .

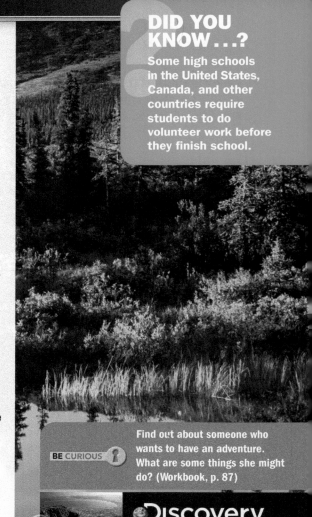

DID YOU KNOW...?

Some high schools in the United States, Canada, and other countries require students to do volunteer work before they finish school.

BE CURIOUS

Find out about someone who wants to have an adventure. What are some things she might do? (Workbook, p. 87)

Discovery EDUCATION

8.3 TIME FOR AN ADVENTURE!

Vocabulary

1. Complete the sentences with the words and phrases.

finish school	get a job
get a driver's license	go to college

1. My sister is going to _go to college_ in Boston next year.

2. You have to take a test before you can _finish school_ and have a car.

3. Amy would like to _get a job_ at a computer design company.

4. I'll _get a driver's_ in May. Then I'm going to work during the summer.

2. Complete the name of each container and the material it is made from.

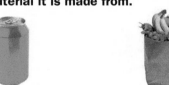

1. M_etal_ C_an_   2. P_aper_ B_ag_

3. G_lass_ J_ar_   4. C_loth_ B_ag_

Grammar

3. Circle be going to for future plans or will for predictions.

Mark: What ¹**will you** / **are you going to** do this summer?

Jenny: My cousin from Canada ²**will** / **is going to** visit us in June, and we ³**will** / **are going to** go on a trip to the mountains.

Mark: Do you think you'll go hiking?

Jenny: Yes, we ⁴**will** / **are**.

Mark: That sounds nice. I think it ⁵**will** / **is going to** be fun.

Jenny: Yeah, I know we ⁶**will** / **are going to** have a good time.

4. Write sentences. Use the present continuous or simple present.

1. we / go / to a restaurant / tonight

We go to a restaurant tonight.

2. the volunteer program / start / on June 15

The volunteer program start on June 15

3. the recycling center / close / at 10:00 p.m. tonight

the recycling center close at 10:00

4. they / get married / in April

They get married in aprill.

Useful language

5. Circle the correct answers.

1. **A:** I think it's a good idea to volunteer somewhere before college.

   B: I suppose you're _____. It's a great experience.

   (a. right)   b. true   c. false

2. **A:** That table made of plastic bottles is cool.

   B: _____. I think it's sort of ugly.

   (a. I agree)   b. I disagree   c. Absolutely

3. **A:** People should retire when they're 60.

   B: _____, but I think some people like to keep working, and that's OK, too.

   a. I disagree   b. Never   (c. Maybe)

4. **A:** I think everyone should recycle plastic, paper, and glass.

   B: _____!

   (a. Absolutely)   b. Never   c. Not now

PROGRESS CHECK: Now I can . . .

- ☐ identify and talk about life events.
- ☐ discuss future plans and predictions.
- ☐ talk about future plans and scheduled events.
- ☐ agree and disagree with someone.
- ☐ write an application letter.
- ☐ talk about places I'd like to volunteer.

9 Watch OUT!

1. What is the teen going to do?

2. Why do you think this is exciting? Do you think it's dangerous?

3. What exciting activities do you or your friends do?

UNIT CONTENTS

Vocabulary Accident and injury verbs; parts of the body

Grammar Present perfect statements with regular and irregular verbs; present perfect questions; present perfect vs. simple past

Listening I'm accident-prone.

Vocabulary: Accident and injury verbs

1. Complete the sentences with the words in the box.

bang	burn	cut	hurt	sprain
break	crash	fall off	slip	✓ trip

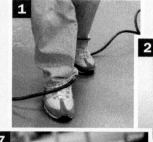

1. We need to move the computer cord, so I don't _____*trip*_____ over it.

2. Be careful! Don't _____ your finger with the knife.

3. If you _____ your leg, you'll have to use crutches.

4. Watch out! You can _____ on the ice.

5. This road is dangerous. Be careful you don't _____ your car.

6. The stove is hot. Don't _____ your hand.

7. Always wear a helmet in case you _____ your bike.

8. Look out! You're going to _____ your head!

9. If you _____ your back, you might need to see a doctor.

10. Put ice on your finger if you _____ it.

 2. Listen, check, and repeat.
9.01

3. Work with a partner. Where are some common places that the accidents and injuries in Exercise 1 happen?

> People often trip over things at school.

> Yes, and they trip over things at home, too.

Speaking: It happened to me!

4. YOUR TURN Work with a partner. When was the last time the accidents and injuries in Exercise 1 happened to you or someone you know?

> I tripped over my dog yesterday!

> My dad cut his finger last week.

 Workbook, p. 58

Reading It's Hard Being a Teen!; Your Invitation; Beware of the Amazon!
Conversation Reacting to good and bad news
Writing An email to refuse an invitation

STAY *Safe!*

It's Hard Being a Teen!

Being a teenager can be difficult – *and dangerous!* The most common injuries for teens are breaking their bones, banging their heads, and getting cuts and burns. Here are some common ways these injuries happen.

Bicycle Accidents

Many teens fall off their bikes. This can cause minor or serious injuries. Many bicycle injuries have happened when teens weren't wearing helmets. If you ride a bike, always wear a helmet!

Car Crashes

Teens have had more car crashes than any other age group. One problem is texting. In the United States, over 30 percent of teens have texted while driving. This causes many accidents. Don't text and drive! And always wear a seatbelt!

Kitchen Accidents

It's easy to cut a finger with a knife. However, burns are the most common kitchen injury. People have burned themselves on the stove or with hot liquids when they weren't careful. Teens need to be careful in the kitchen!

Sports Injuries

Exercise is good for you, but it can also be dangerous. Many teens get injuries when they play sports. Injuries in winter sports, like snowboarding and skiing, are very common. In the past, most snowboarding injuries have happened to people under 30. If you play sports, you'll want to wear protective equipment.

So, be careful and be safe . . . on the street, at home, and on the soccer field!

Reading: Common teen injuries and accidents

1. Work with a partner. Look at the title, subtitles, and photos. What do you think the article is about?

2. Read and listen to the article. Where do teens often get hurt?

3. Read the article again. Check the common injuries and accidents for teens.

Common injuries	Common accidents
☐ spraining their hands	☒ crashing a car
☒ head injuries	☒ falling off a bike
☒ cuts	☐ falling down the stairs
☐ hurting their backs	☒ getting hurt playing a sport
☒ broken bones	☒ burning their hands on a stove
☒ burns	☐ tripping over something

4. **YOUR TURN** Work with a partner. Can you think of other common injuries and accidents?

> Many people bang their heads.

Grammar: Present perfect statements with regular and irregular verbs

5. Complete the chart.

	Affirmative statements	Negative statements
Regular verbs	Liv **has slipped** on the ice many times. Most snowboard injuries _____ **happened** to people under 30.	Kyle _____ **burned** his hand in years. Eva**'s never burned** her hand. They **haven't crashed** a car before. I**'ve** _____ **crashed** a car.
Irregular verbs	Martin _____ **broken** his arm twice. Teens **have had** more crashes than any other age group.	Julia **hasn't cut** her finger before. Teens _____ **worn** helmets. We**'ve never seen** an accident.
Contractions	has = **'s** _____ = **'ve**	

> Check your answers: Grammar reference, p. 114

6. Complete the sentences with the present perfect. The verbs in blue are irregular. Check the correct forms of these verbs on p. 121.

1. I _____ *'ve broken* _____ (broke) my arm before.

2. My parents _____ (travel) to many countries.

3. I _____ (sing) in a band for five years.

4. I _____ (slip) and _____ (fall) on the ice before.

5. My best friend _____ (write) a blog since July.

6. My cousins _____ (live) in Mexico since 2012.

7. My brother _____ (trip) over our cat many times.

8. I _____ (take) a safety class before.

7. Work with a partner. Are the sentences in Exercise 6 true for you? If not, make them negative.

> I've broken my arm before.

> Really? I've never broken my arm.

Speaking: True or false?

8. YOUR TURN Work with a partner. Say two true and two false things you have and haven't done before. Your partner guesses if they are true or false. Take turns.

> I've eaten snake.

> I think that's false.

> No, it's true!

9. Join another pair. Tell the pair what your partner has and hasn't done.

> Dan has eaten snake. He hasn't flown in a plane. He's never . . .

Spell it RIGHT!

Past participles For regular verbs:
+ -**ed**: bang → bang**ed**
+ -**d**: live → live**d**
-**y** → -**i** + -**ed**: study → stud**ied**
double consonant + -**ed**: trip → trip**ped**
For irregular verbs: See p. 121.

Get it RIGHT!

Do not put **never** before the verb. It goes between **has/have** and the past participle in the present perfect.
You **have never broken** your arm.
NOT: ~~You **never have broken** your arm.~~

BE CURIOUS Find out about *E. coli*. What foods can you get *E. coli* from? (Workbook, p. 88)

Discovery EDUCATION

9.1 DANGER IN OUR FOOD

Actions and
ACCIDENTS

Listening: I'm accident-prone.

1. Do you and your friends do any dangerous sports or activities? What are they?

 2. Listen to Angie and Franco talk about accidents and injuries. Who gets hurt easily?

    a. Franco

    b. Angie

    c. both Franco and Angie

 3. Listen again. Are the sentences true (*T*) or false (*F*)?

    1. Angie has broken her arm in the past. ____

    2. She has fallen off her bike. ____

    3. She doesn't wear a helmet when she rides her bike. ____

    4. She fell off a swing when she was a baby. ____

    5. She slipped in the kitchen once. ____

    6. Franco has broken his arm. ____

Vocabulary: Parts of the body

4. Match the words (a–i) with the correct parts of the body. Then listen and repeat.

a. an ankle

b. an elbow

c. a foot

d. a knee

✓ e. a neck

f. a shoulder

g. a stomach

h. toes

i. a wrist

1. [e]
2. [ ]
3. [ ]
4. [ ]
5. [ ]
6. [ ]
7. [ ]
8. [ ]
9. [ ]

5. What other parts of the body do you know? Make a list.

> *eyes, a head, fingers . . .*

6. **YOUR TURN** Work with a partner. Tell your partner what parts of the body you've injured. Use these verbs and your own ideas.

| break | burn | cut | hurt | sprain |

> I've broken my wrist, and I've sprained my knee.
> I've also burned my fingers.

NOTICE IT
The plural of *foot* is *feet*.

Grammar: Present perfect questions; present perfect vs. simple past

7. Complete the chart.

Use the present perfect to ask questions about experiences that happened at an indefinite time in the past. Ever is often used in Yes/No questions.

Yes/No questions	Wh- questions
Have you **ever broken** an arm? Yes, I _____. / No, I **haven't**.	What bones _____ you **broken**? My wrist, my arm, and my leg.
_____ she **ever fallen** off her bike? Yes, she **has**. / No, she _____.	Why **has** she **had** accidents? Because she's clumsy.

Remember: Use the simple past, not the present perfect, for experiences that happened at a definite time in the past.

Have you ever fallen off your bike?	Yes, I have. I **fell** off my bike yesterday.
What happened the second time?	I **slipped** and **fell**. I **broke** my wrist.

> Check your answers: Grammar reference, p. 114

8. Write questions with the present perfect. The verbs in blue are irregular. Check the correct forms of these verbs on p. 121.

1. you / ever / lose / your keys   *Have you ever lost your keys?*

2. your parents / ever / live / in another city   _____

3. your / best friend / fall off / a bike   _____

4. you / ever / slip on something   _____

5. what bones / you / break   _____

6. where / your teacher / travel   _____

9. Work with a partner. Ask and answer the questions in Exercise 8.

> Have you ever lost your keys?

> Yes, I have.

10. Circle the correct words.

1. (It's stopped) / It stopped raining. Let's ride our bikes.
2. **I've never tried / I didn't try** snowboarding. I'd love to do that.
3. My mom **has read / read** a good book last week.
4. When **have you hurt / did you hurt** your foot?
5. My brother **has banged / banged** his knee a lot. He's accident-prone.

Say it RIGHT!

In *Wh-* questions, **have** often sounds like /əv/. Listen to the questions.

*Where **have** you been?*
*What **have** you seen?*

Pay attention to the way you pronounce **have** in Exercise 11.

Speaking: Have you ever . . . ?

11. YOUR TURN Work with a partner. Ask and answer questions in the present perfect. Use the phrases from the box or your own ideas. Add additional information in the simple past.

climb a mountain	have a pet	try an adventure sport	try Mexican food

> Have you ever tried an adventure sport?

> Yes, I have.

> What sport have you tried?

> I went globe riding two years ago. I loved it!

A Dangerous TRIP?

Conversation: Good news, bad news

 9.06

1. **REAL TALK** Watch or listen to the teenagers. Check the accidents and injuries they've had.

☐ broken an arm   ☐ cut a foot   ☐ fell out of a tree   ☐ tripped over a skateboard
☐ broken a leg   ☐ cut a hand   ☐ sprained a wrist
☐ burned a hand   ☐ fell off a bike   ☐ sprained an ankle

2. **YOUR TURN** Have *you* ever had an accident? Tell your partner.

 9.07

3. Holly is telling Theo some news. Listen and complete the conversation.

USEFUL LANGUAGE: Reacting to good and bad news

| I'm sorry to hear that. | That's too bad. | That sounds like fun. | That's cool! |

Theo: Hi, Holly. How's it going?

Holly: Well . . . I have good news, and I have bad news.

Theo: What happened?

Holly: I'll start with the bad news. I **fell on a ski trip** and **sprained my ankle**.

Theo: ¹_____ So, what's the good news?

Holly: I met a new friend at the hospital. She's really nice.

Theo: ²_____ But, what happened to her?

Holly: She **tripped over some shoes** and **broke her arm**.

Theo: Oh, no! ³_____

Holly: I know. But we've texted each other a lot, and we're **going to the beach** this weekend.

Theo: ⁴_____

4. Practice the conversation with a partner.

5. **YOUR TURN** Repeat the conversation in Exercise 3, but change the words in purple. Use the information in the chart for one conversation and your own ideas for another.

		My ideas
First accident	fell off my skateboard at a competition	
First injury	cut my leg	
Second accident	slipped on the stairs	
Second injury	hurt her knee	
Activity	seeing a movie	

To: TedR12@middleschool.cup.org
From: garytruss@net.cup.org
Subject: Your invitation

Hi Ted,

Thanks for inviting me to the amusement park on Saturday. I'm sorry, but I can't go with you. My family is going on a trip with real danger. We're going to swim with sharks this weekend! Have you ever done that?

I've taken diving classes for two years. I've been on a lot of dives, but I've never seen sharks. Actually, it will be safe. We're going with a diving instructor, and we'll be in cages. But it's still scary! Look at the photo I sent from the diving website.

Again, I'm really sorry. Have a great time! Maybe we can go to the amusement park together in July.

Your friend,

Gary

Reading to write: An email to refuse an invitation

6. **Look at the photo. What do you think Gary is going to do? Read his email to check.**

 Focus on **CONTENT**
When you refuse an invitation:
- thank the person for the invitation
- apologize at the beginning of the note
- explain why you can't accept the invitation
- apologize again at the end of the note
- suggest another time to do something

7. **Read Gary's email again. Why can't he go to the amusement park? When does he suggest going to the amusement park with Ted?**

 Focus on **LANGUAGE**
You can use these phrases to refuse an invitation.
To thank someone:
Thanks for inviting me to . . .
Thank you for the invitation to . . .
To apologize and refuse:
I'm sorry, but I . . .   *I'd love to come, but . . .*
Sorry, but I'm busy . . .   *I'm really sorry.*
To suggest another time:
Could we go . . . ?   *Maybe we can . . .*
How about another time?

8. **Which phrases in the Focus on Language box does Gary use in his email?**

9. **Circle the correct words.**

   [1]**Thanks / Sorry** for the invitation to your pool party. [2]**Maybe we can / I'd love to** come, but I broke my leg last week. I can't get my cast wet, and the doctor said I have to stay off my leg for several weeks.
   I'm really [3]**busy / sorry**. I hope you have a great birthday and party. [4]**How about / Thanks for** another time? [5]**Sorry / Maybe** I can come over and swim in a few months.

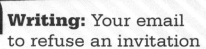 **Writing:** Your email to refuse an invitation

○ **PLAN**
Your friend invited you to an event, and you can't go. Write notes about it with your own ideas.

The event	
Why you can't go	
Another time you could go	

○ **WRITE**
Write your email. Use your notes to help you. Write at least 80 words.

○ **CHECK**
Check your writing. Can you answer "yes" to these questions?

• Is information for each category from the Focus on Content box in your email?

• Do you use expressions from the Focus on Language box correctly?

BEWARE OF THE AMAZON!

Millions of people have visited the Amazon rain forest, and more will visit in the future. They have seen tiny insects, beautiful birds, and playful monkeys. But some Amazon animals are very dangerous!

HOME | Virtual Tour | About Us | Contact Us | FAQs

BRAZILIAN WANDERING SPIDERS aren't very big, but they are very dangerous! Some say they are the most poisonous spiders in the world! Don't let this scary creature bite your hands or feet.

As you can tell from the name, **POISON DART FROGS** are also poisonous. They don't bite, but these cute and colorful frogs have poisonous skin. Their bright colors tell other animals, "Watch out! I'm poisonous. Don't eat me!" The golden poison dart frog is only about five centimeters long, but its skin has enough poison to kill 10 people!

ANACONDAS aren't small. They're very big snakes, and they never stop growing. People have seen anacondas up to 6.5 meters long. They aren't poisonous, but they are definitely dangerous. They squeeze animals and then eat them whole! People have found birds, pigs, and jaguars in their stomachs!

JAGUARS are big and beautiful cats, and they can kill. They are the third biggest cat in the world, after lions and tigers. They eat more than 80 different kinds of animals. They've even eaten anacondas!

So, who would win a fight between an anaconda and a jaguar? Either animal could win. But it's the tiny **MOSQUITO** that is the most dangerous animal in the rain forest. You can become very sick or even die from a mosquito bite.

Watch out for these dangerous Amazon animals - big and small!

Culture: Dangerous rain forest animals

1. **Look at the title and the photos. How do you think these animals are similar? How are they different?**

2. **Read and listen to the article. Which Amazon animals are small? Which ones are big?**

3. **Read the article again. Answer the questions.**
   1. Which animals are poisonous? _____
   2. Why is the poison dart frog's skin colorful? _____
   3. What are some animals that anacondas have eaten? _____
   4. Which cats are bigger than jaguars? _____
   5. Which animal is the most dangerous? _____

4. **YOUR TURN** **Work with a partner. What are some dangerous animals in your country? What do you know about them? Have you or has someone you know ever had an experience with a dangerous animal?**

DID YOU KNOW...?
Some people in the Amazon use the poison from the poison dart frog's skin in blow darts. They use the darts to hunt and kill other animals.

BE CURIOUS
Find out about some animals in Australia. Which ones are dangerous? (Workbook, p. 89)

Discovery
EDUCATION

9.3 A DEADLY JOB

Vocabulary

1. Match the warnings with the situations.

1. The floor is wet. ___
2. That box is heavy. ___
3. The pan is hot. ___
4. This knife is very sharp. ___
5. That trail has a lot of rocks on it. ___
6. There's a book on the floor. ___
7. The ceiling is low. ___
8. The road is dangerous. ___

a. Don't fall off your bike.
b. Don't bang your head.
c. Don't hurt your back.
d. Don't crash your car.
e. Don't slip!
f. Don't cut your finger.
g. Don't trip!
h. Don't burn your hand.

2. Write the name for each part of the body.

1. _____
2. _____
3. _____
4. _____
5. _____
6. _____
7. _____
8. _____
9. _____

Grammar

3. Write negative sentences two ways.

1. I / not slip / on ice *I haven't slipped on ice.*
   I've never slipped on ice.

2. Jake / not burn / his arm
   _____
   _____

3. we / not fall / off our bikes
   _____
   _____

4. my parents / not crash / their car
   _____
   _____

5. you / not hurt / your back
   _____
   _____

4. Complete the conversation with the present perfect or the simple past.

Jim: ¹_____ you ever _____ (be) scuba diving?

Lia: No, I ²_____. Have you?

Jim: Yes, I ³_____. I ⁴_____ (go) scuba diving last week.

Lia: Cool! ⁵_____ you _____ (like) it?

Jim: Yes. I ⁶_____ (love) it!

Lia: I ⁷_____ never _____ (do) any adventure sports.

Jim: Do you want to?

Lia: Not really.

Useful language

5. Circle the correct words.

1. **A:** I fell off a ladder last week.

   B: That sounds like fun. / That's too bad. Are you OK?

2. **A:** I'm going to the Amazon rain forest next month.

   B: That's cool! / That's too bad!

3. **A:** My mother slipped and broke her arm.

   B: I'm sorry to hear that. / That's cool.

4. **A:** My family is going to go hiking this weekend.

   B: I'm sorry to hear that. / That sounds like fun.

PROGRESS CHECK: Now I can . . .

☐ talk about accidents and injuries.
☐ talk about things I have and haven't done.
☐ ask, answer, and give details about things I've done.

☐ react to good and bad news.
☐ write an email to refuse an invitation.
☐ talk about dangerous animals.

10 Have Fun!

BE CURIOUS

A New York City Food Tour

How do you celebrate your birthday?

Punkin Chunkin!

An Ancient Answer

1. Where are the teens?

2. What are they doing? Are they having fun?

3. What do you do for fun?

UNIT CONTENTS

Vocabulary Free-time activities; adjectives of feeling
Grammar Indefinite pronouns; *too* and *enough*
Listening I'll never forget . . .

Vocabulary: Free-time activities

1. Label the pictures with the correct phrases.

celebrate your birthday	have a party	play video games	spend time with your family
go to a dance	listen to music	read books	take photos
✓ hang out with friends	play an instrument		

1. _____

2. _____

3. _____

4. _____

5. _____

6. _____

7. *hang out with friends* and _____

8. _____ and _____

2. Listen, check, and repeat.

10.01

3. Work with a partner. Where do you usually do the activities in Exercise 1? Are there any activities you don't do?

> I listen to music alone in my room. I don't go to dances.

Speaking: Top 5

4. YOUR TURN Work with a group. What are your top five favorite activities from Exercise 1? Which one is the most popular with the group?

> My top five favorite activities are taking photos, celebrating . . .

> Workbook, p. 64

Reading Jodi's Blog; Your Invitation; April Fool's!
Conversation Making and responding to suggestions
Writing An invitation

Weekend **FUN**

JODI'S BLOG

I want to go somewhere fun this weekend. I'll go anywhere in the city or close by. Does anyone have a good idea? Please post a picture if you have one!

VERONICA RAMIREZ

Go to the outdoor community swimming pool. It's a great place to spend time with your family or hang out with friends. There's something for everyone there! You can swim, sit in the sun and read a book, or go to the café for a snack. I always have a good time there!

MIKE BENSON

Why don't you listen to music on Saturday – live music! I'm in a band with my friends, and we're playing at Roks Café at 9:00 p.m. We all play different instruments. I play the drums, my friend Joe plays the piano, and Cassandra plays the guitar and sings. Come and listen to us and bring someone with you. Hey – if anyone knows about future gigs, we'll play anywhere! ☺

JASON PETERS

You could go power kiting in the park. It's a cool, new sport, and it's a lot of fun! I went last weekend, and I've never done anything like it before. It's a combination of skateboarding and kite flying. It looks hard, but it's actually pretty easy. The guide helps you with everything and even takes your photo while you're in the air!

DID YOU KNOW...?

The world's largest outdoor swimming pool is in Chile. It's more than 1 km long. That's the size of 20 Olympic swimming pools.

Reading: Weekend plans

1. **Work with a partner. Look at the photos. Which activity looks like the most fun?**

2. **Read and listen to the article. What does each person suggest for Jodi?**

   10.02

3. **Read the article again. Who does or did these things? Check (✓) the correct names. Sometimes more than one answer is possible.**

	Veronica	Mike	Jason
does an outdoor activity			
spends time with his/her family			
plays an instrument			
does a sport			
does an activity with friends			

4. **YOUR TURN** **Work with a partner. What fun things can you do on the weekend in your city or in other areas?**

> You can go to an amusement park and . . .

Grammar: Indefinite pronouns

5. Complete the chart.

Use indefinite pronouns for people, places, and things that are not specific.

	People	**Places**	**Things**
some-	_____	somewhere	something
every-	everyone	everywhere	_____
no-	no one	nowhere	nothing
any-	anyone	_____	anything
	Bring **someone** with you.	I want to go **somewhere** fun.	He helps you with **everything**.
	No one has an idea.	We'll play **anywhere**.	I've never done **anything** like it.

> Check your answers: Grammar reference, p. 115

6. Replace the underlined words with an indefinite pronoun.

1. I think there's a̶ ̶p̶e̶r̶s̶o̶n̶ *someone* at the door.

2. Where's Jack? He's <u>in a room</u> in the house, I think.

3. I've looked for my bag <u>in all the places</u> in my room. I can't find it <u>in any place</u>.

4. There's <u>no food</u> in the fridge.

5. Ouch! I have <u>a small object</u> in my shoe!

6. There's <u>not one place</u> to listen to music in this town.

7. Circle the correct words.

Edinburgh, Scotland, is an amazing city. ¹(**Anyone**) / **Anything** could have fun there. It's the world capital of festivals. There's a festival for ²**everything / everywhere**, and there's always ³**something / somewhere** to do. In the summer, it has the biggest arts festival in the world. There are thousands of events ⁴**everything / everywhere** in the city. Many of the outdoor shows are free. In the winter, the Scottish New Year party is a three-day festival that ⁵**everything / everyone** goes to. ⁶**Nowhere / No one** wants to miss it! If you don't have ⁷**nothing / anything** better to do this summer, go to Edinburgh!

Speaking: Fun in my town

8. **YOUR TURN** **Work with a partner. Think of the following things for your town.**

> an area where there's nothing to do
> a place everyone likes to go
> a place no one likes to go
> a place that sells everything for computers
> a place you can buy anything you need
> someone famous from your town
> something to do on the weekend
> somewhere to play sports

> Clinton Park is somewhere you can play sports.

> So is City Stadium.

Get it **RIGHT!**

Use indefinite pronouns with **any-**, not **no-**, in negative sentences.
I **didn't show anyone** the photo.
NOT: ~~I didn't show no one the photo.~~
I **didn't go anywhere** on vacation.
NOT: ~~I didn't go nowhere on vacation.~~
I **didn't do anything** with my friends.
NOT: ~~I didn't do nothing with my friends.~~

BE CURIOUS Find out about food in New York City. What is something each restaurant is famous for? (Workbook, p. 90)

Discovery EDUCATION

10.1 A NEW YORK CITY FOOD TOUR

Exciting
TRIPS

Listening: I'll never forget . . .

1. Have you ever been on an interesting or exciting school trip? What did you do?

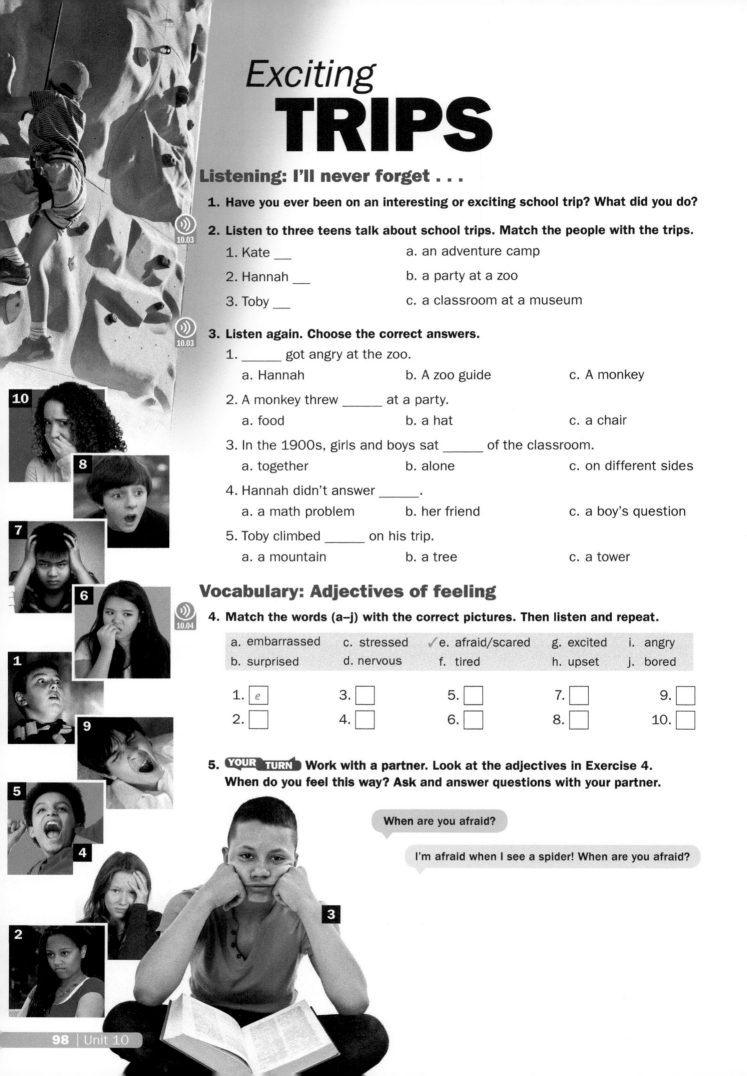

2. Listen to three teens talk about school trips. Match the people with the trips.

   1. Kate ___   a. an adventure camp

   2. Hannah ___   b. a party at a zoo

   3. Toby ___   c. a classroom at a museum

3. Listen again. Choose the correct answers.

   1. _____ got angry at the zoo.
      a. Hannah   b. A zoo guide   c. A monkey

   2. A monkey threw _____ at a party.
      a. food   b. a hat   c. a chair

   3. In the 1900s, girls and boys sat _____ of the classroom.
      a. together   b. alone   c. on different sides

   4. Hannah didn't answer _____.
      a. a math problem   b. her friend   c. a boy's question

   5. Toby climbed _____ on his trip.
      a. a mountain   b. a tree   c. a tower

Vocabulary: Adjectives of feeling

4. Match the words (a–j) with the correct pictures. Then listen and repeat.

   | a. embarrassed | c. stressed | ✓e. afraid/scared | g. excited | i. angry |
   | b. surprised | d. nervous | f. tired | h. upset | j. bored |

   1. [e]   3. [ ]   5. [ ]   7. [ ]   9. [ ]
   2. [ ]   4. [ ]   6. [ ]   8. [ ]   10. [ ]

5. **YOUR TURN** Work with a partner. Look at the adjectives in Exercise 4.
   When do you feel this way? Ask and answer questions with your partner.

   When are you afraid?

   I'm afraid when I see a spider! When are you afraid?

Grammar: *too* and *enough*

6. Complete the chart.

> Use *too* + adjective + infinitive to show something is more than what we want or need.
> Use adjective + *enough* + infinitive to show something is what we want or need. Not
> *enough* shows something is less than we want or need.

too	enough
I was **too scared** _____ **answer**.	I was **strong** _____ **to do** it.
They were _____ **nervous to try** something.	The monkey was**n't big enough** _____ **reach** the food.

> Check your answers: Grammar reference, p. 115

7. Complete the sentences with *too* + adjective + infinitive.

angry	cold	✓ scared	stressed	tired

1. Yolanda is _too scared to watch_ (watch) the horror movie!

2. I don't want to go in the water because it's _____ (swim).

3. We rode bikes all morning. We're _____ (go) on a hike.

4. You're _____ (talk) to me now. Call me when you're calmer.

5. Jeff is _____ (have) fun; he needs to relax.

8. Complete the sentences with (*not*) *enough* + the adjectives and verbs.

1. We can't have a picnic because it's _not warm enough to eat_ (warm / eat) outside.

2. Lilly is _____ (young / get) into the museum for free. She has to buy a ticket.

3. I was _____ (tired / fall) asleep on the train. I missed my stop!

4. My sister is _____ (old / drive). Maybe she can take us to the mall.

5. I'm _____ (tall / reach) my suitcase. Can you get it for me, please?

9. Circle the correct words.

1. Don't go in the ocean. It's **not dangerous enough / (too dangerous)** to swim.

2. I'm going to bed. I'm **tired enough / too tired** to watch TV.

3. Victor was sick yesterday, but he's **well enough / too well** to go to school today.

4. You can't move that box. You're **not strong enough / too strong**.

5. Jan is **not embarrassed enough / too embarrassed** to sing in the musical.

Speaking: Are you old enough?

10. **YOUR TURN** Work with a partner. Use these phrases to describe yourself or someone you know.

(not) hungry enough to . . .   too embarrassed to . . .

(not) old enough to . . .   too scared to . . .

(not) strong enough to . . .   too tired to . . .

> I'm not old enough to drive.

> My little brother's too scared to go snowboarding.

Say it **RIGHT!**

The letters **gh** can be silent or make the /f/ sound. They make the /f/ sound in **enough**. Listen to the sentence.

/haɪ/ /ɪnʌf/

*The ladder isn't **high enough** to reach the window.*

Pay attention to the way you pronounce **enough** in Exercise 10.

> Workbook, pp. 66–67

Let's CELEBRATE!

REAL TALK | 10.2 HOW DO YOU CELEBRATE YOUR BIRTHDAY?

Conversation: Birthday plans

10.06

1. **REAL TALK** Watch or listen to the teenagers. How do, did, or will they celebrate their birthdays? Number the activities in the order you hear them.

___ took an exam	___ has a big party
___ is going to have a dance party	___ had a pink party
___ prefers to celebrate at home	___ goes on a trip

2. **YOUR TURN** How do *you* celebrate *your* birthday? Tell your partner.

10.07

3. Molly and Paul are talking about birthday plans. Listen and complete the conversation.

USEFUL LANGUAGE: Making and responding to suggestions

I'd rather	That's a great idea!	How about	Why don't we

Molly: What should we do for your birthday?

Paul: I don't know. I want to have a party and do something fun.

Molly: OK. Who are you inviting?

Paul: My **friends and a few people in my family.**

Molly: ¹_____ **go to the beach**? We can **have a picnic.**

Paul: ²_____ do something more exciting.

Molly: OK. Let's see . . . we could **go to the water park.**

Paul: Hmm . . . I've done that several times before. I want to do something really different.

Molly: Hey, here's an idea . . . ³_____ **paintball**?

Paul: ⁴_____ Everyone will like that.

Molly: Great. I'll email the invitations.

Paul: Cool. Thanks.

4. **Practice the conversation with a partner.**

5. **YOUR TURN** Repeat the conversation in Exercise 3, but change the words in purple. Use the information in the chart for one conversation and your own ideas for another.

		My ideas
Who you're inviting	my cousins and my best friend	
First suggestion	go to the mountains	
Activity for first suggestion	go horseback riding	
Second suggestion	ice-skating	
Third suggestion	miniature golf	

To: LolaP@net.cup.org
From: sara98@net.cup.org
Subject: An invitation

Hi Lola,

How were your exams? I'm glad to be done with <u>them</u>. I did well enough to pass, but the math and history <u>ones</u> were really hard.

Anyway, I'm having a party to celebrate the end of the school year, and I'd like you to come. It's on June 23 at Mario's Restaurant. It's the <u>one</u> behind the movie theater. We're meeting <u>there</u> at 7:00 p.m. We'll have pizza and listen to live music after dinner.

I invited 20 people. I hope <u>everyone</u> can come! The room is big enough for 25 people, so you can invite a friend.

On Thursday, I have to tell the restaurant how many people are coming. Please let me know by <u>then</u> if you can come.

Your friend,

Sara

Reading to write: An invitation

6. Look at the photo. What do you think Sara is inviting Lola to do? Read Sara's email to check.

> *Focus on* **CONTENT**
> When you write an invitation:
> - give the event
> - give the reason for the event
> - give the details of the event
> - ask for a response

7. Read Sara's email again. What is the event? Why is she having it? Where and when is it? What activities will there be?

> *Focus on* **LANGUAGE**
> You can use *referencing words* when you don't want to repeat a noun.
> Pronouns:
> *I bought **a guitar**, but I haven't learned to play **it**.*
> One/Ones:
> *You take great **photos**. I like the black and white **ones**.*
> Then:
> *Joe's birthday is on **Friday**. I need to buy him a gift. I hope I have time to buy something before **then**.*
> There:
> *We're meeting at the **ice-skating rink**. See you **there**!*

8. What nouns do the underlined referencing words in Sara's email refer to?

9. Circle the correct words.

1. I need a new book to read. Can you suggest any good **them / ones**?

2. I like to hang out with friends at The Get Away Café. Have you been **it / there**?

3. I have six cousins. I love to spend time with **them / then**.

4. Here's an invitation to my party. I'm sorry I didn't give **it / then** to you sooner.

 Writing: Your invitation

○ **PLAN**
You are going to invite your friend to a fun event. Think of an event and write notes about it.

Why _____   When _____

The Event _____

Where _____   What Activities _____

○ **WRITE**
Write your invitation. Use your notes to help you. Write at least 80 words.

○ **CHECK**
Check your writing. Can you answer "yes" to these questions?

- Is information for each category from the Focus on Content box in your invitation?

- Do you use referencing words correctly?

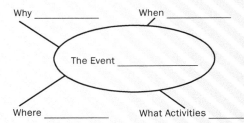

APRIL FOOLS!

Be careful! Today is April 1. Don't listen to your friends when they say school's closed for a week. Don't run to the window if your brother tells you it's snowing. And don't believe everything you see on TV and the Internet.
It's April Fool's Day, and you don't want to be a fool!

April Fool's Day probably began in the 1500s in France when New Year's Day moved from April 1 to January 1. Of course, there wasn't any TV or Internet then, so some people didn't know about this change. People called anyone who still celebrated New Year's Day on April 1 a fool.

Playing jokes on April 1 became popular, and in the 1700s, this tradition spread to England, Scotland, and eventually the United States. Today, people celebrate April Fool's Day in many countries around the world. News shows and Internet sites enjoy the fun, too!

A British TV station has made many April Fool's jokes. In 1957, it showed a program about spaghetti growing on trees. A lot of people thought it was true and called the station to ask where they could buy the trees. In 1980, reporters said that Big Ben, the famous clock in London, had a new digital face. Everyone was angry until the reporters told them it was an April Fool's joke!

An Internet company is also famous for its April Fool's Day jokes. In 2014, it advertised a keyboard for cats to use so they could type on computers. That same year, the company said it was making a "magic hand" – a robot that types on your cell phone for you. Both inventions were jokes!

Have you ever been foolish enough to believe an April Fool's Day joke?

Culture: April Fool's Day

1. **Look at the photos. What do you see? Which ones do you think are pictures of real things?**

2. **Read and listen to the article. Which is NOT an April Fool's Day joke in the article?**
   a. A clock gets a digital face.
   b. You can buy a keyboard for your cat.
   c. You can smell things on the Internet.
   d. Spaghetti grows on trees.

3. **Read the article again. Choose the correct answers to the questions.**
   1. On April Fool's Day, people _____.
      a. don't go to school   b. play jokes on each other   c. have a party
   2. Before the 1500s, New Year's Day was on _____.
      a. April 1   b. January 1   c. two different days
   3. _____ believed the joke about spaghetti growing on trees.
      a. Everyone   b. No one   c. Some people

4. **YOUR TURN** **Work with a partner. Think of two April Fool's Day jokes to tell people.**

   > We can tell people that monkeys can talk.

   > Yes. And we can make a video . . .

BE CURIOUS — Find out about a pumpkin-throwing competition. What are the rules? (Workbook, p. 91)

Discovery EDUCATION

10.3 PUNKIN CHUNKIN!

Vocabulary

1. Label the pictures with the correct phrases.

celebrate a birthday	play video games
go to a dance	read books
listen to music	take photos

1. _____

2. _____

3. _____

4. _____

5. _____

6. _____

2. Complete the sentences.

| angry | nervous | tired |
| embarrassed | scared | |

1. Susan's really _____. She went to bed late last night.

2. Tim is _____ of spiders, especially the big ones!

3. Nina is _____ about playing in her first concert tonight.

4. Julie's teacher was very _____ because Julie was late for class again.

5. Brett was _____ because he forgot his grandma's birthday.

Grammar

3. Complete the sentences with the words in parentheses and -one, -thing, or -where.

1. I like _____ (every) in this store. I want to buy it all!

2. We didn't see Ken _____ (any).

3. _____ (every) at the park had fun.

4. There is _____ (no) to eat here.

4. Complete the sentences with enough or too + adjectives and verbs.

1. I'm _____ (scared / go) into the ocean.

2. We're not _____ (strong / lift) that box.

3. He felt _____ (sick / go) to school this morning.

4. My brother runs _____ (fast / win) the race.

Useful language

5. Complete the conversation.

| How about | I'd rather | That's a great idea | Why don't we |

Shel: What do you want to do today?

Andy: ¹_____ horseback riding?

Shel: I don't think so. ²_____ do something inside.

Andy: OK. ³_____ go to the mall?

Shel: ⁴_____! We can shop and then eat lunch.

PROGRESS CHECK: Now I can . . .

☐ talk about free-time activities.

☐ talk about weekend plans.

☐ describe feelings and situations with *too* and *enough*.

☐ make and respond to suggestions.

☐ write an invitation.

☐ talk about April Fool's Day and jokes.

▶ REVIEW UNITS 9–10, Workbook, pp. 70–71

CLIL PROJECT

10.4 An Ancient Answer, p. 120

Uncover Your Knowledge

UNITS 6–10 Review Game

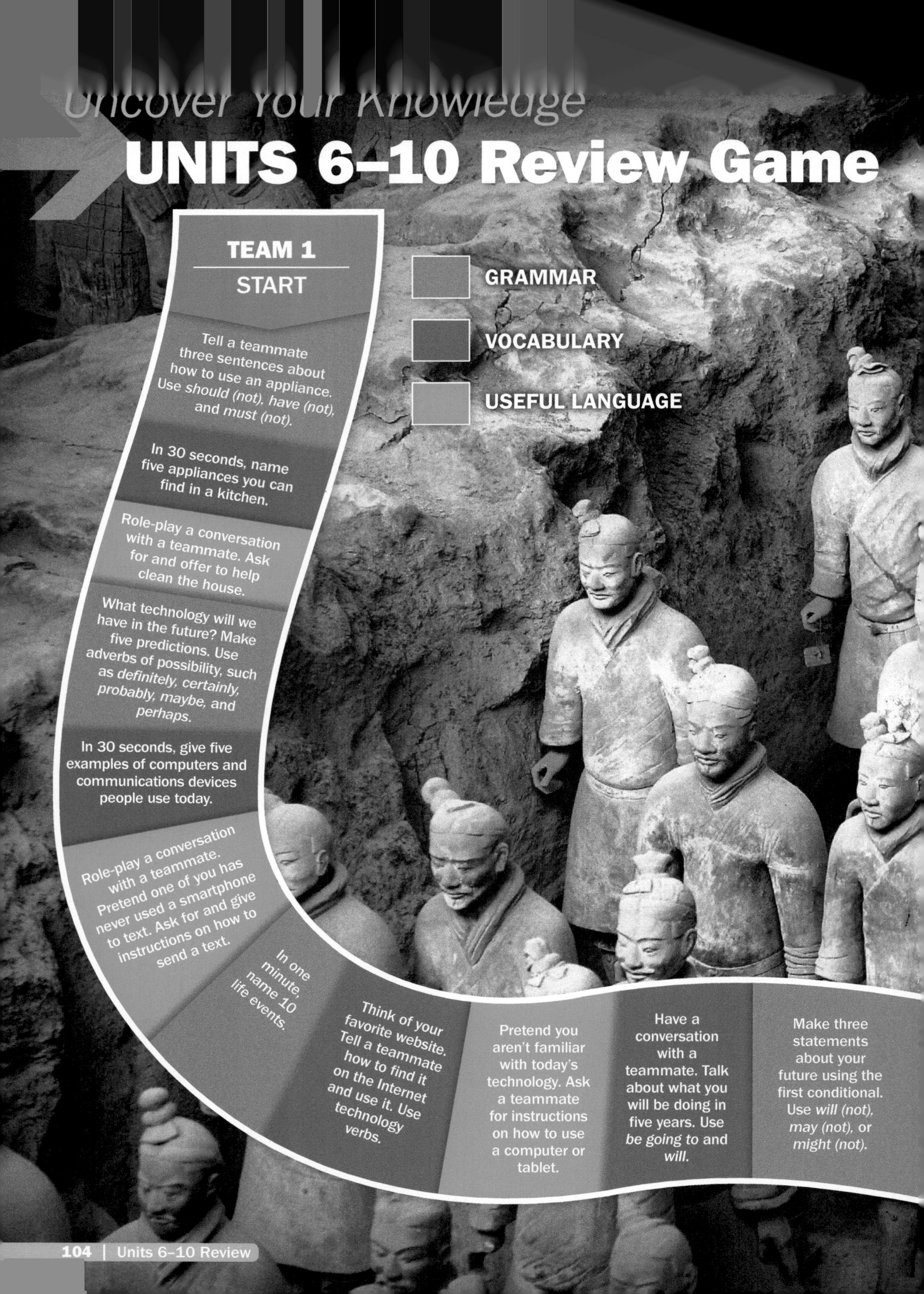

TEAM 1
START

Tell a teammate three sentences about how to use an appliance. Use *should (not)*, *have (not)*, and *must (not)*.

In 30 seconds, name five appliances you can find in a kitchen.

Role-play a conversation with a teammate. Ask for and offer to help clean the house.

What technology will we have in the future? Make five predictions. Use adverbs of possibility, such as *definitely, certainly, probably, maybe,* and *perhaps*.

In 30 seconds, give five examples of computers and communications devices people use today.

Role-play a conversation with a teammate. Pretend one of you has never used a smartphone to text. Ask for and give instructions on how to send a text.

In one minute, name 10 life events.

Think of your favorite website. Tell a teammate how to find it on the Internet and use it. Use technology verbs.

Pretend you aren't familiar with today's technology. Ask a teammate for instructions on how to use a computer or tablet.

Have a conversation with a teammate. Talk about what you will be doing in five years. Use *be going to* and *will*.

Make three statements about your future using the first conditional. Use *will (not)*, *may (not)*, or *might (not)*.

GRAMMAR

VOCABULARY

USEFUL LANGUAGE

TEAM 2
START

Role-play a conversation with a teammate. For every suggestion about something to do, offer a counter-suggestion. See how long you can keep the conversation going.

Role-play with a teammate. Act out five different feelings, and your teammate guesses the adjective.

Role-play a conversation with a teammate. Take turns telling each other about an accident or injury you had. Use expressions like *That's too bad* or *I'm sorry to hear that* to react to the bad news.

Tell a teammate six of your favorite free-time activities.

Give clues using indefinite pronouns to get your teammate to name a person, a place, or a thing (for example, *it's something many people enjoy watching: this year it will take place somewhere fun.*)

Play good news/bad news. Tell a teammate something good or bad that happened. Your teammate has to respond quickly to the news. See how many you can say in two minutes.

Point to and name nine parts of the body.

Ask a teammate four questions about his/her past. Use the question *Have you ever . . . ?* Your teammate answers.

With a teammate, make three statements about the environment and recycling. Agree and disagree with each other.

In 30 seconds, name five ways someone can get hurt. Use accident verbs.

Use the present continuous to ask a teammate about his/her future plans. Then use the simple present to ask when the events will happen.

How can you agree or disagree in a conversation? Give two examples of each.

INSTRUCTIONS:

■ Make teams and choose game pieces.

■ Put your game pieces on your team's START.

■ Flip a coin to see who goes first.

■ Read the first challenge. Can you do it correctly?

    Yes → Continue to the next challenge.

    No → Lose your turn.

The first team to do all of the challenges wins!

Simple present review with *be* and *have*, p. 5

Use the simple present of be *to identify people and give locations and dates.*
Use the simple present of have *to talk about possessions, characteristics, and relationships.*

be	have
Wh- questions and answers	
Where **am** I? You**'re** in Quito. You**'re not** in Otavalo.	Where **do I have** art class? You **have** art in room 9. You **don't have** art in room 10.
Where **are** you? I**'m** in Otavalo. I**'m not** in Quito.	When **do** you **have** art class? I **have** art at 10:00. I **don't have** art at 9:00.
How old **is** he/she/it? He**'s**/She**'s**/It**'s** 14. He**'s**/She**'s**/It**'s not** 17.	What **does** he/she/it **have** for dinner? He/She/It **has** meat. He/She/It **doesn't have** fish.
Who **are** we/they? We/They **are** Maria's parents. We**'re**/They**'re** her grandparents.	What do we/they **have**? We/They **have** a computer. We/They **don't have** a desk.
Yes/No questions and answers	
Am I in Quito? Yes, you **are**. / No, you **aren't**.	**Do I have** art in room 9? Yes, you **do**. / No, you **don't**.
Are you in Otavalo? Yes, I **am**. / No, I**'m not**.	**Do** you **have** art at 10:00? Yes, I **do**. / No, I **don't**.
Is he/she/it 14? Yes, he/she/it **is**. / No, he/she/it **isn't**.	**Does** he/she/it **have** meat for dinner? Yes, he/she/it **does**. / No, he/she/it **doesn't**.
Are we/they Maria's parents? Yes, we/they **are**. / No, we/they **aren't**.	**Do** we/they **have** a computer? Yes, we/they **do**. / No, we/they **don't**.

1. Complete the sentences with the correct form of *be* or *have*. Write affirmative sentences for items with a ✔. Write negative sentences for items with an X.

1. We _____ dinner at 6:00 p.m. (✔)
2. Lydia _____ 17 years old. (✔)
3. Dan and Lia _____ a music class. (X)
4. You _____ my sister. (X)
5. _____ they at school? (✔)
6. When _____ she _____ lunch? (✔)

whose and possessives, p. 7

Use whose *to ask about possession.*
Use a name/noun + 's, a possessive adjective, or a possessive pronoun to show possession.

Whose	Possessive 's or s'
Whose computer is it? / **Whose** is it?	It's Dad**'s** computer.
Whose shoes are they? / **Whose** are they?	They're our grandmother**'s** shoes.
Whose house is that? / **Whose** is that?	That's our grandparents**'** house. That's Lois**'s** house.
Possessive adjectives	**Possessive pronouns**
It's **my/your/his/her/our/their** computer.	It's **mine/yours/his/hers/its/ours/theirs**.
They're **my/your/his/her/our/their** shoes.	They're **mine/yours/his/hers/its/ours/theirs**.
That's **my/your/his/her/its/our/their** house.	That's **mine/yours/his/hers/its/ours/theirs**.

2. Circle the correct words to complete the sentences.

1. This photo is **my / mine**.
2. **Who's / Whose** car is that?
3. I have **Sheila's / hers** pen.
4. **Yours / Your** phone is small.
5. That house is **our / ours**.
6. Look at **their / theirs** faces.

Simple present review, p. 15

Use the simple present to talk about routines, habits, and facts.

Wh- questions	Affirmative answers	Negative answers
What movies **do** you **like**?	I **like** horror movies.	I **don't like** musicals.
How often **does** he/she **go** to the movies?	He/She **goes** to the movies three times a week.	He/She **doesn't go** to the movies on Sundays.
Yes/No questions	Short answers	
Do you **like** horror movies?	Yes, I/we **do**.	No, I/we **don't**.
Does he/she **go** to the movies?	Yes, he/she **does**.	No, he/she **doesn't**.
Contractions do not = **don't**	does not = **doesn't**	

1. Complete the conversation with the simple present.

Dan: Hey, Jim. ¹ _Do_ you _work_ (work) at the movie theater on Elm Street?

Jim: Yes, I ² _____ .

Dan: ³ _____ it _____ (show) animated movies?

Jim: Yes, it ⁴ _____ . There is one there now, *Super Kid*. Why?

Dan: My brother ⁵ _____ (like) animated movies. Let's all go see it!

Jim: OK. When?

Dan: On Sunday. My brother ⁶ _____ (study) in the morning, so let's go at noon.

Jim: Great. I ⁷ _____ (not work) on Sundays.

Verb + infinitive or *-ing* form (gerund), p. 17

Verb + infinitive	Verb + gerund
have, hope, need, plan, want	*dislike, don't mind, enjoy, finish*
They **want to watch** a drama.	Sheldon **dislikes trying** new things.
He **needs to see** who gets voted off *Big Brother*.	Leonard **enjoys trying** different things.
I **plan to go** to a movie on Saturday.	We **don't mind watching** commercials.
Verb + infinitive or *-ing* form (gerund)	
hate, like, love, prefer, start	
I **like to read** comic books. I **like reading** comic books.	
They **love to read** comic books. They **love reading** comic books.	
She **hates to watch** reality TV shows. She **hates watching** reality TV shows.	
He **prefers to get** the news online. He **prefers getting** the news online.	

2. Put the words in the correct order to make sentences. Use the infinitive or gerund form of the underlined word. Sometimes more than one answer is possible.

1. about documentaries / <u>read</u> / we / like

   We like to read about documentaries . OR *We like reading about documentaries* .

2. <u>work</u> / Denny / at 6:00 / finishes

   _____

3. starts / in the afternoon / it / often / <u>rain</u>

   _____

4. after school / hopes / <u>watch</u> / her favorite show / Ann

   _____

5. movies / <u>watch</u> / on my computer / hate / I

   _____

Present continuous review; simple present vs. present continuous, p. 25

Use the present continuous to talk about activities that are happening now.

Wh- questions	Affirmative answers	Negative answers
What **am** I **doing**?	You**'re playing** soccer.	You**'re not playing** baseball.
What **are** you **doing**?	I**'m writing** about my life.	I**'m not writing** about my job.
What **is** he/she **doing**?	He/She **is skating**.	He/She **isn't running**.
What **are** we/they **doing**?	We/They **are watching** the fish.	We/They **aren't skating**.

Yes/No questions	Short answers	
Am I **playing** soccer?	Yes, you **are**.	No, you **aren't**.
Are you **writing** about Dubai?	Yes, I **am**.	No, I**'m not**.
Is he/she **skating**?	Yes, he/she **is**.	No, he/she **isn't**.
Are we/they **shopping**?	Yes, we/they **are**.	No, we/they **aren't**.

Remember: Use the simple present for facts, habits, and routines.

At night, the water **changes** color. = routine
Look! The water **is changing** color. = activity happening now

1. **Circle the correct words to complete the sentences.**

   1. Margot **shop / shops / is shopping / are shopping** in a sporting goods store right now.

   2. Dan and Eduardo **play / plays / is playing / are playing** soccer every Saturday.

   3. Where **do / does / am / are** you usually **go / goes / going / to go** after class?

   4. **Do / Does / Is / Are** she **buy / buys / buying / to buy** a tablet right now?

   5. We **eat / eats / am eating / are eating** at the food court in the mall now.

   6. **Do / Does / Is / Are** Lexi usually **buy / buys / buying / to buy** her books online?

Quantifiers, p. 27

Use quantifiers to show the amount of something.

With countable plural nouns	With uncountable nouns
How **many** T-shirts do you have?	How **much** money do you have?
I have **some / a lot of / enough** T-shirts.	I have **some / a lot of / enough** money.
I don't have **many / any / a lot of / enough** T-shirts.	I don't have **much / any / a lot of / enough** money.
Are there **many / any / a lot of / enough** T-shirts in your dresser?	Is there **much / any / a lot of / enough** money in your bank account?
Yes, there are. / No, there aren't.	Yes, there is. / No, there isn't.

2. **Circle the correct words to complete the conversation.**

   A: Do you have [1]**many / any** money I can borrow?

   B: Yes, I do. How [2]**many / much** money do you need?

   A: I need [3]**any / enough** money to buy books for my class.

   B: How [4]**many / much** books do you need?

   A: I need [5]**a lot of / much** books! About 10.

   B: Well, how [6]**many / much** do they cost?

   A: I think about $300 in total.

   B: Oh, OK. Well, I can't lend you $300, but I can lend you [7]**enough / some** money. It's [8]**not a lot of / not enough**, but I can lend you $100.

   A: A: That really helps. Thanks! I can pay you back in two weeks.

Simple past statements review and *ago*, p. 35

Use simple past statements to describe things in the past and to talk about past events and activities.
Use *ago* to say how far back in the past something happened or was.

	Affirmative statements	Negative statements
be	I/He/She **was** MVP in 2011.	I/He/She **wasn't** MVP in 2010.
	They/We/You **were** in Brazil a week **ago**.	They/We/You **weren't** in Spain last week.
Regular verbs	I/He/She/They/We/You **played** for Mexico.	I/He/She/They/We/You **didn't play** for Spain.
	I/He/She/They/We/You **moved** a month **ago**.	I/He/She/They/We/You **didn't move** last week.
Irregular verbs	I/He/She/They/We/You **made** a solo album in 2003.	I/He/She/They/We/You **didn't make** an album in 2001.
	I/He/She/They/We/You **got** a tablet a year **ago**.	I/He/She/They/We/You **didn't get** a laptop.

For regular verbs:	+ -*ed*: work → work**ed**	+ -*d*: live → live**d**
	-*y* → -*i* + -*ed*: try → tr**ied**	double consonant + -*ed*: shop → shop**ped**

For irregular verbs: See p. 121.

1. Write statements in the simple past.

1. we / win / two medals a year ago   *We won two medals a year ago.*

2. Dennis / grow up / in Guatemala   _____

3. Cassie / be / Player of the Year in 2014   _____

4. my friends / not sing / at the party last night   _____

5. you / be / funny at the party last weekend   _____

Simple past questions review and *ago*, p. 37

Use simple past questions to ask about past things, events, and activities.
Use *ago* to ask how far back in the past something happened or was.

	Wh- questions and answers	*Yes/No* questions and answers
be	How **was** he/she an hour **ago**? He/She **was** happy.	**Was** he/she happy an hour **ago**? Yes, he/she **was**. / No, he/she **wasn't**.
	Where **were** they/we? They/We **were** at home.	**Were** they/we/you at home? Yes, they/we/you **were**. / No, they/we/you **weren't**.
Regular verbs	How long **ago did** I/he/she/it/they/we/you **start**? I/He/She/It/They/We/You **started** an hour **ago**.	**Did** I/he/she/it/they/we/you **start** an hour **ago**? Yes, I/he/she/it/they/we/you **did**. / No, I/he/she/it/they/we/you **didn't**.
	Why **did** I/he/she/they/we/you **carry** him? I/He/She/They/We/You **carried** him because he was hurt.	**Did** I/he/she/they/we/you **carry** him? Yes, I/he/she/they/we/you **did**. / No, I/he/she/they/we/you **didn't**.
Irregular verbs	What **did** I/he/she/they/we/you **see**? I **saw** a fire.	**Did** I/he/she/they/we/you **see** a fire? Yes, I/he/she/they/we/you **did**. / No, I/he/she/they/we/you **didn't**.
	Where **did** I/he/she/they/we/you **put** the ladder? I/He/She/They/We/You **put** it against the house.	**Did** I/he/she/they/we/you **put** the ladder against the house? Yes, I/he/she/they/we/you **did**. / No, I/he/she/they/we/you **didn't**.

2. Write questions for the answers.

1. **A:** _____*Where did you go last night?*_____   **B:** I went to a soccer game.

2. **A:** _____   **B:** I saw a famous writer at the restaurant.

3. **A:** _____   **B:** No, I wasn't at the concert. I was at home.

4. **A:** _____   **B:** Yes, I did. I studied for two hours last night.

5. **A:** _____   **B:** I wrote about my aunt because I admire her.

Past continuous, p. 45

Use the past continuous to talk about activities that were in progress in the past.

Wh- questions	Affirmative answers	Negative answers
Who **was** I **talking** to?	You **were talking** to the butler.	You **weren't talking** to the maid.
What **were** you **doing**?	I **was talking** on the phone.	I **wasn't talking** to Max.
What **was** he/she **reading**?	He/She **was reading** a newspaper.	He/She **wasn't reading** a book.
What **were** they/we **doing**?	They/We **were playing** tennis.	They/We **weren't playing** soccer.
Yes/No questions	Short answers	
Was I **talking** to the teacher?	Yes, you **were**.	No, you **weren't**.
Were you **talking** to Max?	Yes, I **was**.	No, I **wasn't**.
Was Max **reading**?	Yes, he **was**.	No, he **wasn't**.
Were they **playing** tennis?	Yes, they **were**.	No, they **weren't**.

1. Complete the questions and answers with the past continuous.

1. **A:** What _____ you _____ (do) last night at 9:00 p.m.?

   B: I _____ (listen) to music, but I _____ (not listen) to it loudly.

2. **A:** _____ Rosa _____ (watch) a detective show this afternoon?

   B: No, she _____. She _____ (clean) her bedroom.

3. **A:** _____ they _____ (chasing) their dog at 8:00 a.m.?

   B: Yes. They _____ (chase) it in the park, but they _____ (not run) very fast.

4. **A:** _____ you _____ (study) for the science test yesterday?

   B: Yes, I _____. I _____ (work) with Jorge.

Simple past vs. past continuous; *when* and *while*, p. 47

Use the past continuous for an event that was in progress.
Use the simple past for an event that interrupted the event in progress.
Use when *or* while *with the phrase in the past continuous.*
Use when *with the phrase in the simple past.*

I was studying (event in progress)	**when** I **saw** red lights in the sky. (event that interrupts)
While/When I **was studying**, (event in progress)	I **saw** red lights in the sky. (event that interrupts)
When it happened, (event that interrupts)	my parents **were sleeping**. (event in progress)
It **happened** (event that interrupts)	**while/when** my parents **were sleeping**. (event in progress)

2. Circle the correct words to complete the sentences.

1. Don **took / was taking** photos when a thief **stole / was stealing** his camera.

2. The phone **rang / was ringing** while Britney **watched / was watching** TV.

3. When the detective **entered / was entering** the room, the maid **cleaned / was cleaning** the house.

4. While I **read / was reading** about Easter Island, someone **knocked / was knocking** on the door.

5. Someone **screamed / was screaming** loudly when Sara and Maria **walked / were walking** their dog.

Comparative and superlative adjectives and adverbs, p. 57

Use comparative adjectives and adverbs to show how two things are different from each other.
Use superlative adjectives and adverbs to compare three or more things.

	Comparative	Superlative
Adjectives	dark → dark**er** big → big**ger**	dark → **the** dark**est** big → **the** big**gest**
	powerful → **more** powerful	popular → **the most** popular
	good → **better** bad → **worse**	good → **the best** bad → **the worst**
	The Rio Negro is **darker** than the Rio Solimões.	The bathroom is **the darkest** room in the hotel.
Adverbs	fast → fast**er** slowly → **more** slowly	fast → **the** fast**est** slowly → **the most** slowly
	far → far**ther**	far → **the farthest**
	well → **better** badly → **worse**	well → **the best** badly → **the worst**
	The Rio Solimões runs **more slowly than** the Rio Negro.	The water runs **the most slowly** in the summer.

1. Complete the sentences with comparative or superlative adjectives or adverbs.

1. My bedroom is *smaller than* (small) my sister's room.

2. Ramon fits _____ (well) in that chair than his father does.

3. We all eat quickly in my family, but my older brother eats _____ (quickly).

4. We stayed at _____ (bad) hotel in the city.

5. I run _____ (fast) my brother.

6. Scott is _____ (powerful) player on the team.

should (not), (not) have to, must (not), p. 59

Use should (not) for advice and recommendations. Use have to for responsibilities.
Use not have to for things that are not required. Use must for obligation. Use must not for prohibition.

Affirmative	Negative
You **should wash** dark clothes separately.	You **shouldn't wash** darker clothes with lighter ones.
She **should look** at the labels.	She **shouldn't put** it in a sunny room.
You **have to choose** the temperature first.	You **don't have to wash** it by hand.
It **has to be** cool.	It **doesn't have to be** cold.
You **must use** cold water.	You **must not (mustn't) use** hot water.
They **must follow** the directions.	They **must not (mustn't) miss** a step.

2. Complete the conversations with *should (not), (not) have to*, or *must (not)* and the verb.

stay

1. You _____ in the Hotel Flores. It's wonderful!

2. Carla _____ in a hotel on her trip. She's staying with a friend.

3. We _____ in a hotel downtown. It's really dangerous.

put

4. I _____ the dishes in the dishwasher before I go out.

5. She _____ her full name on the form. She's not allowed to use a nickname.

6. You _____ that information on the Internet. It's against the law.

will and *won't* for predictions, p. 67

Use will *and* won't *to predict future events.*

Wh- questions	Affirmative answers	Negative answers
What **will** my smartphone **do** in the future?	Perhaps it**'ll think** like a human.	It **won't drive** a car.
How **will** you/I/he/she/it/they/we **change**?	You/I/He/She/It/They/We **will be** smaller.	You/I/He/She/It/They/We **won't be** bigger.
Yes/No questions	**Short answers**	
Will my smartphone **think** like a human?	Yes, it **will**.	No, it **won't**.
Will you/I/he/she/it/they/we **change**?	Yes, you/I/he/she/it/they/we **will**.	No, you/I/he/she/it/they/we **won't**.

Contractions	I will = I'll	you will = you'll	he will = he'll	she will = she'll	it will = it'll
	we will = we'll		they will = they'll		

1. Complete the sentences with *will* or *won't* and the verbs in parentheses.

1. Where _____ you _____ (live) in the future?

2. Computers _____ (be) faster in five years.

3. We _____ (not buy) big phones in the future.

4. _____ Janelle _____ (study) computer science?

5. Most people _____ (not use) keyboards in a few years.

First conditional with *will (not)*, *may (not)*, and *might (not)*, p. 69

Use the first conditional to show results or possible results of future actions. Use if *and the simple present in the main clause, and* will (not), may (not), *or* might (not) *and the base form of a verb in the result clause.*

Statements
You**'ll see** all of the choices **if** you **zoom out**.
If I **make** games, they **won't be** boring.
If I **ask** my parents, they **might get** it for me for my birthday.
I **may not get** the Ztron 2100 **if** a new model **comes** out.
Questions
What kind of games **will** you **make if** you**'re** a designer?   Action games.
If I **beat** you, **will** you **do** my homework?   Yes, I **will**. / No, I **won't**.

2. Write sentences in the first conditional with the phrases in the box.

Main clause	Result
1. I / take / the bus / to school	I / might / be / late
2. John / buy / a computer	he / will not / get / a tablet
3. you / zoom out	you / will / see / the entire town
4. Mia and Sara / share / a computer	they / may not / finish / their homework
5. I / back up / my files	I / will not / worry

1. _____

2. _____

3. _____

4. _____

5. _____

be going to and *will*, p. 77

> Use be going to *to talk about plans in the future.*
> Use will *to talk about predictions and unplanned decisions.*

be going to	will
Wh- questions and answers	
What **are** you/we/they **going to do**? I'**m**/We'**re**/You'**re**/They'**re going to study** agriculture. He/She/It **is not going to study** history.	Where **will** you/I/he/she/it/we/they **live**? I/You/He/She/It/We/They **will live** in the outback. I/You/He/She/It/We/They **won't live** in Sydney.
Yes/No questions and answers	
Are you/we/they **going to go** to Sydney? Yes, I **am**. / Yes, we/you/they **are**. No, I'**m**/we'**re**/you'**re**/they'**re not**. **Is** he/she/it **going to study** history? Yes, he/she/it **is**. / No, he/she/it **isn't**.	**Will** you/I/he/she/it/we/they **stay** here? Yes, you/I/he/she/it/we/they **will**. No, you/I/he/she/it/we/they **won't**.

1. Write questions for the answers. Use *be going to* or *will*.

1. **A:** (when / you / study) _____

   B: I'm going to study after school.

2. **A:** (they / get married / in March) _____

   B: Yes, they will.

3. **A:** (we / drive / to the library) _____

   B: No, we aren't.

4. **A:** (where / Lea / go / to college) _____

   B: She'll go to the University of Chicago.

Present continuous and simple present for future, p. 79

> As with be going to, *use the present continuous to talk about future plans.*
> Use the simple present to talk about scheduled future events.

Present continuous	Simple present
Wh- questions and answers	
What **are** you/they/we **doing** next week? I'**m**/We'**re**/You'**re**/They'**re (not) collecting** trash.	What time **do** I/you/they/we **start**? I/We/You/They **start** at 9:00 a.m. tomorrow. I/We/You/They **don't start** at 9:00 a.m. tomorrow.
Why **is** he/she **going** there? He'**s**/She'**s taking** a year off. He'**s**/She'**s not traveling**.	When **does** he/she **start** the project? He/She **starts** next week. He/She **doesn't start** tomorrow.
Yes/No questions and answers	
Are we/you/they **helping** the turtles? Yes, we/you/they **are**. No, we'**re**/you'**re**/they'**re not**.	**Do** I/you/they/we **start** at 9:00 a.m. tomorrow? Yes, I/you/they/we **do**. No, I/you/they/we **don't**.
Is he/she **taking** a year off? Yes, he/she **is**. No, he/she **isn't**.	**Does** he/she/it **start** in five minutes? Yes, he/she/it **does**. No, he/she/it **doesn't**.

2. Circle the correct words.

1. John **is working / works** on an eco-project next summer.

2. Carla and Sammy **are making / make** jewelry from old metal cans tomorrow.

3. The store **is opening / opens** at 10:00 a.m. tomorrow.

4. **Is the class starting / Does the class start** at noon on Monday?

5. Where **are they going / do they go** tomorrow?

Present perfect statements with regular and irregular verbs, p. 87

Use the present perfect to talk about experiences that happened at an indefinite time in the past.
Use has/have + the past participle to form the present perfect.

	Affirmative statements	Negative statements
Regular verbs	He/She/It **has slipped** on the ice many times. Most snowboard injuries **have happened** to people under 30. I/We/They/You **have crashed** a car.	He/She **hasn't burned** his/her hand in years. He/She **has never burned** his/her hand. I/We/They/You **haven't crashed** a car before. I/We/They/You **have never crashed** a car.
Irregular verbs	He/She/It **has broken** his/her/its arm twice. I/You/We/They **have had** more crashes than any other age group.	He/She **hasn't cut** his/her finger before. Teens **haven't worn** helmets. I/You/We/They **have never seen** an accident.

Contractions   has = **'s**   have = **'ve**

1. **Circle the correct words.**

   1. Marcy **has had / has have** three broken bones.

   2. Ronaldo **has gone / has went** on many exciting vacations.

   3. We **have slip / have slipped** on ice in front of our house.

   4. **I've haven't seen / I've never seen** an anaconda before.

   5. She **haven't burned / hasn't burned** her finger.

Present perfect questions; present perfect vs. simple past, p. 89

Use the present perfect to ask questions about experiences that happened at an indefinite time in the past. Ever is often used in Yes/No questions.

Yes/No questions	Wh- questions
Have I/you/we/they **ever broken** an arm? Yes, I/you/we/they **have**. No, I/you/we/they **haven't**.	What bones **have** I/you/we/they **broken**? My wrist, my arm, and my leg.
Has he/she **ever fallen** off his/her bike? Yes, he/she **has**. / No, he/she **hasn't**.	Why **has** he/she/it **had** accidents? Because he/she/it is clumsy.
Remember: Use the simple past, not the present perfect, for experiences that happened at a definite time in the past.	
Have you ever fallen off your bike? What happened the second time?	Yes, I have. I **fell** off my bike yesterday. I **slipped** and **fell**. I **broke** my wrist.

2. **Circle the correct answers.**

   1. Have you ever ___ off your bike?

      a. fall   b. fell   c. fallen

   2. Elsa ___ a poison dart frog at the museum yesterday.

      a. saw   b. has seen   c. has saw

   3. ___ you snowboard in the mountains on your trip?

      a. Do   b. Did   c. Have

   4. What bones ___ you broken?

      a. did   b. has   c. have

   5. Luke ___ his cousins in months.

      a. didn't see   b. hasn't seen   c. haven't seen

Indefinite pronouns, p. 97

Use indefinite pronouns for people, places, and things that are not specific.

	People	Places	Things
some-	**someone** Bring **someone** with you.	**somewhere** I want to go **somewhere** fun.	**something** I see **something** in the water.
every-	**everyone** I invited **everyone** in my class.	**everywhere** Lilly takes her phone **everywhere**.	**everything** He helps you with **everything**.
no-	**no one** **No one** has an idea.	**nowhere** Jason is **nowhere** to be found.	**nothing** We have **nothing** ready for the party.
any-	**anyone** Does **anyone** have a good idea?	**anywhere** We'll play **anywhere**.	**anything** I've never done **anything** like it.

1. Complete the sentences with *some-, every-, no-,* or *any-* + the word in parentheses.

1. I looked _____ (where) in my room for my keys.

2. _____ (one) came to the party because Ted put the wrong date on the invitation.

3. Kate didn't say _____ (thing) about the party, so I was really surprised.

4. I have _____ (thing) to do on Saturday, but I can meet you on Sunday.

5. We are _____ (where) near Jeff's house. How did we get so lost?

6. _____ (one) is at the door, but I don't know who it is.

too and *enough*, p. 99

Use too + adjective + infinitive to show something is more than want we want or need.
Use adjective + enough + infinitive to show something is what we want or need.
Not enough shows something is less than we want or need.

too	enough
I/He/She was **too scared to answer**.	I/He/She was **strong enough to do** it. You/They/We were **old enough to know** better.
You/They/We were **too nervous to try** something.	I/He/She/It was**n't big enough to reach** the food. You/They/We were**n't tall enough to get** on the ride.

2. Circle the correct word to complete each sentence.

1. Vinny is **too / enough** excited to sleep.

2. Melanie is good **too / enough** to play on the team.

3. It's **too / enough** hot to play outside.

4. My parents aren't old **too / enough** to retire.

5. Are you bored **too / enough** to leave the party?

6. It isn't **too / enough** late to see a movie.

ROBOTS *in the Real* WORLD

1. **Complete the sentences with the correct words.**

communicate	computer	create	design	machine	professor	teacher

1. A ___PROFESSOR___ is a higher-level ___teacher___ in a university.

2. A ___compu___ is a thinking ___Machine___. It can ___commdnl___ with other ones.

3. To ___Design___ something is to make or draw plans for it. Next, you ___create___ it.

2.4 WHO'S REAL?

2. **Watch the video. Are the sentences true (T) or false (F)?**

1. Professor Ishiguro is wearing a blue shirt. __F__ ✓

2. The robot is wearing a watch. __T__ ✓

3. Professor Ishiguro's first name is Hitoshi. __F__ ✓

4. One of the three students is a woman. __F__ ✓

5. They sit at a round table. __T__ ✓

6. The white robot can run and turn around. __T__ ✓

3. **Complete the paragraph with the correct words.**

color	glasses	hair	move	same	shy	strange	think	twins

Look at these two men. What looks the ¹ ___same___ ? What looks different? Now look at their faces and look at their ² ___hair___ . It's the same ³ ___color___ , isn't it? And they both have ⁴ ___glasses___. So what do you ⁵ ___think___ ? Are they ⁶ ___twins___ ? OK, now watch how they ⁷ ___move___ . What's ⁸ ___shy___ here? This man isn't talking. Is he very ⁹ ___strange___ ?

 PROJECT **Plan your own robot – what do you want your robot to do? Answer the questions below. Then draw or make a model of your robot. Show your robot to the class and tell them about it.**

- What three things do you want your robot to do for you?

- Do you think you will enjoy life with a robot? Why or why not?

- What do you think robots will do in the next few years?

- Will robots make life better or worse for people? Why?

Unsolved **MYSTERIES**

1. **Amelia Earhart was a famous female pilot from the United States. Label the places from Amelia's last flight.**

| Howland Island | Lae, Papua New Guinea | North Africa | Pacific Ocean | South America | South Asia |

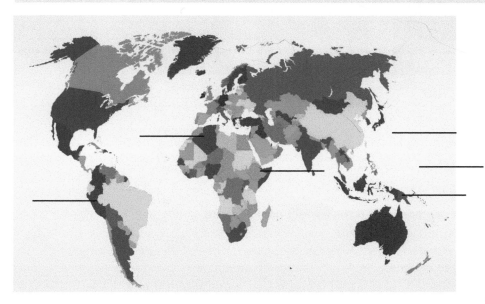

2. **Watch the video. Number the sentences in the order that you hear them from 1–6.**

_____ a. Next, they went across North Africa and South Asia.

_____ b. She was one of the first female pilots.

_____ c. She traveled with a navigator.

_____ d. We are on the line 157–337.

_____ e. In 2001, a team looked for clues.

_____ f. But the island was very small and difficult to find.

Discovery
EDUCATION
4.4 AMELIA EARHART: FAMOUS FLYER

PROJECT **Here are some famous mysteries. Choose the most interesting one and find out more about it. Write an explanation of what you think happened.**

MYSTERY: Sailors found the ship *Mary Celeste* abandoned with one lifeboat missing
WHEN: December 1872
WHERE: Atlantic Ocean, near Africa
FACTS: Weather was good, plenty of food and water on ship
WHAT HAPPENED?

MYSTERY: Building Stonehenge
WHEN: 3000–2000 BCE
WHERE: The south of England
FACTS: Made from stones weighing 45 tons from 40 kilometers away and stones weighing almost 4 tons from 390 kilometers away
WHAT HAPPENED?

MYSTERY: The Yeti, a large animal, like an ape
WHEN: First spotted in the 1800s
WHERE: The Himalayas, in Nepal and Tibet
FACTS: Many people believe it exists, but there are no photographs of it.
WHAT HAPPENED?

Life below the **SURFACE**

1. Label the pictures with the correct words.

diver   storyteller   Tokyo   tower   Yonaguni

1 _____ **2** _____ **3** _____ **4** _____ **5** _____

Discovery EDUCATION

5.4 AN UNDERWATER MYSTERY

2. Watch the video. Complete the sentences with the correct conjunctions.

and   but   so   when

1. Not many people live on these islands, _____ it's quiet and calm.

2. Yonaguni is part of Japan, _____ it has its own language and culture.

3. In the 1980s, he was diving near the island of Yonaguni _____ he found something amazing.

4. It had streets, steps, _____ tall towers.

3. Are the sentences true (*T*) or false (*F*)?

1. Yonaguni is to the north of Japan. _____

2. About a hundred people live on Yonaguni. _____

3. The people here tell old stories to their children. _____

4. Kihachiro Aratake is a driver. _____

5. It looked like a large city under the water. _____

6. Some scientists think the structure was once above the water. _____

PROJECT

Do you know the story of the Lost City of Atlantis? Some people believe Atlantis was an underwater city, like the structures around Yonaguni.

Find out more about Atlantis and complete the chart below. Then compare the stories of Atlantis and Yonaguni and make a presentation about these two places.

	Atlantis	Yonaguni
Possible location(s)?		*off the coast of Japan*
When did the city exist?		*10,000 years ago*
What do people believe happened to the city?		
What do you believe?		

Wonders of the **WORLD**

1. Label the pictures with the correct words.

Cairo   stone blocks   tomb   pyramid

1 _____   **2** _____   **3** _____   **4** _____

2. Watch the video. Complete the sentences with the correct numbers.

2   3   8   20   147

a. There are _____ giant pyramids near Cairo.

b. _____ million people live in Cairo.

c. People worked for _____ years to build each pyramid.

d. The pyramid of Khufu is _____ meters tall.

e. There are _____ million stone blocks in this pyramid.

Discovery EDUCATION

7.4 THE SECRET OF THE PYRAMIDS

3. Circle the correct answers.

1. They are called the pyramids of _____.

   a. Cairo
   b. Giza
   c. Khufu

2. The builders covered the top of the tallest pyramid with _____.

   a. gold
   b. silver
   c. paint

3. Each stone block weighs as much as _____.

   a. a small car
   b. a large car
   c. a bus

4. The pyramids were _____.

   a. homes
   b. castles
   c. tombs

People started building the Seven Wonders of the World more than 4,000 years ago. The only one still standing is the Pyramid of Khufu. What are the names of the other six Wonders of the World?

Choose one of the Seven Wonders of the World and find out seven interesting facts about it. Create a poster of your Wonder and present it to your class.

Inventions from the **PAST**

1. Look at this picture of a step well. What do you think it does? Label the picture with the correct words:

arches   roof   stairs   walkway

1. _____

2. _____

3. _____

4. _____

10.4 AN ANCIENT ANSWER

2. Watch the video. Are the sentences true (*T*) or false (*F*)?

1. In northern India, the monsoon season lasts for six months every year. _____

2. Step wells are a system for collecting water. _____

3. People built step wells to collect water when it rained. _____

4. People still build step wells today. _____

5. The animals don't get enough water. _____

3. How did people build step wells? Number the events in order 1–5.

_____ a. They cut steps into the earth.

_____ b. They made a hole near the tree.

_____ c. They looked for a tall tree.

_____ d. They covered these steps with stones.

_____ e. They made the hole wider at the top.

PROJECT **Read the list below. Number the inventions and discoveries from what you think are the least important (1) to the most important (10).**

_____ the wheel   _____ clothes

_____ rope   _____ houses

_____ musical instruments   _____ fire

_____ the boat   _____ knives

_____ paint   _____ spears

Then imagine selling one of these inventions to your classmate. How will it make his or her life better? Write three reasons your classmate should buy your invention.

Irregular verbs

Base Verb	Simple Past	Past Participle
be	was, were	been
become	became	become
break	broke	broken
bring	brought	brought
build	built	built
buy	bought	bought
catch	caught	caught
choose	chose	chosen
come	came	come
cut	cut	cut
do	did	done
draw	drew	drawn
drink	drank	drunk
drive	drove	driven
eat	ate	eaten
fall	fell	fallen
feel	felt	felt
find	found	found
fit	fit	fit
fly	flew	flown
forget	forgot	forgotten
get	got	gotten
give	gave	given
go	went	gone
grow	grew	grown
hang	hung	hung
have	had	had
hear	heard	heard
hide	hid	hidden
hold	held	held
hurt	hurt	hurt
keep	kept	kept
know	knew	known
leave	left	left

Base Verb	Simple Past	Past Participle
lend	lent	lent
lose	lost	lost
make	made	made
meet	met	met
pay	paid	paid
put	put	put
read	read	read
ride	rode	ridden
ring	rang	rung
run	ran	run
say	said	said
see	saw	seen
sell	sold	sold
send	sent	sent
shut	shut	shut
sing	sang	sung
sit	sat	sat
sleep	slept	slept
speak	spoke	spoken
spend	spent	spent
stand	stood	stood
steal	stole	stolen
swim	swam	swum
take	took	taken
teach	taught	taught
tell	told	told
think	thought	thought
throw	threw	thrown
understand	understood	understood
wear	wore	worn
win	won	won
withdraw	withdrew	withdrawn
write	wrote	written

Answer to p. 44 #4 (Who stole the painting?)

The butler and Ray stole the painting. The butler told Clarissa there was a phone call. When she went to answer, he stayed in the garden and then climbed through the living room window. He took the painting and came back out through the window. He passed it to Ray. Ray climbed over the wall and gave it to someone waiting in the street.

Credits

The authors and publishers acknowledge the following sources of copyright material and are grateful for the permissions granted. While ever̶̶̶̶̶ ̶̶̶̶̶ ̶̶̶̶̶ ̶̶̶̶̶en made, it has not always been possible to identify the sources of all the material used, or to trace all copyright holders. If any omissions are brought to our notice, we w̶̶̶̶̶ ̶̶̶̶̶ ̶̶̶̶̶ ̶̶̶̶̶o include the appropriate acknowledgements on reprinting.

p. 2-3 (B/G): Getty Images/Lonely Planet Images; p. 3 (a): Alamy/© Imagebroker/Klaus-Werner Friedrich; p. 3 (b): Alamy/©Radius Images; p. 3 (c): Shutte̶ ̶ ̶ ̶mages/Melis; p. 3 (d): Getty Images/Chicago History Museum; p. 3 (e): Shutterstock Images/Gurgen Bakhshetsyan; p. 3 (f): Alamy/©2d Alan King; p. 3 (g): Getty Images/Retrofile/Ge̶ ̶ ̶ ̶arks; p. 3 (h): Shutterstock Images/Ferenc Szelepcsenyi; p.3 (i): Alamy/©Bon Appetit; p. 3 (j): Shutterstock Images/Subbotina Anna; p. 3 (k): Alamy/©Greg Vaughn; p. 3 (l): Alamy/©̶ ̶ ̶il Gordon/Danita Delimont; p. 4 (BL): Corbis/Guillermo Granja; p. 4 (BR): Alamy/©Mo Fini; p. 4 (TR): Alamy/©Maria Grazia Casella; p. 5 (BR): Shutterstock Images/Blend Images; p. 6 (TL) ̶Shutterstock Images/Jenoche/A; p. 6 (a): Shutterstock Images/James Steidl; p. 6 (b): Alamy/©Old Paper Studios; p. 6 (c): Shutterstock Images/Nataliya Hora; p. 6 (d): Shutterstock ̶A̶ ̶ommunications Ltd; p. 6 (e): Shutterstock Images/Marc Dietrich; p. 6 (f): Alamy/©Yvette Cardozo; p. 6 (g): Getty Images/De Agostini; p. 6 (h): Alamy/©Museum of London; ̶ ̶ ̶ ̶ck Images/Balefire; p. 6 (j): Shutterstock Images/Rob Stark; p. 8 (BR): Shutterstock Images/PhotoNan; p. 8 (CL): Shutterstock Images/Doomu; p. 9 (TR): Getty Im̶ ̶ ̶ ̶Digital Vision; p. 10 (B/G): Shutterstock Images/illustrart; p. 10 (TL): Getty Images/Joe Petersburger; p. 10 (TC): Getty Images/GDT; p. 10 (B): Alamy/©Chris ̶ ̶ ̶mageDB; p. 11 (CR): Shutterstock Images/Manczurov; p. 11 (TL): Shutterstock Images/AlexMaster; p. 11 (TR): Shutterstock Images/Zybr78; p. 11 (CL)̶ ̶ ̶ ̶Filippo; p. 11 (CR): Shutterstock Images/WBB; p. 11 (BR): Alamy/©Urbanmyth; p. 11 (BL): Shutterstock Images/Samuel Borges Photography; p. 12-13 (B/G): Getty Im̶ ̶ ̶ ̶): Getty Images/Movie Poster Image Art; p. 13 (2): Alamy/©AF Archive; p. 13 (3): ©DISNEY CHANNEL/THE KOBAL COLLECTION; p. 13 (4): REX/Courtesy Everett Collection; ̶ ̶ ̶ ̶Everett; p. 13 (6): Alamy/©Moviestore Collection; p. 13 (7): ©20TH CENTURY FOX/PARAMOUNT/THE KOBAL COLLECTION; p. 13 (8): REX/Courtesy Everett Co̶ ̶ ̶ ̶Alamy/©AF Archive; p. 14 (T): Shutterstock Images/Bertrand Benoit; p. 14 (B/G): Shutterstock Images/Krivosheev Vitaly; p. 14 (CL): Alamy/©AF Archive; p. 14 (C): THE KOBAL C̶ ̶ ̶ ̶/LUCASFILM/20TH CENTURY FOX; p. 14 (CR): Alamy/©Moviestore Collection Ltd; p. 15 (CR): Getty Images/Adrian Weinbrecht; p. 16 (TL): Shutterstock Images/Szocs Jozsef; p. 16 (1): Getty Images/Jasin Boland/NBC/NBCU Photo Bank; p. 16 (2): Alamy/©Jochen Tack; p. 16 (3): Getty Images/Steve Mort/AFP; p. 16 (4): Alamy/©AF Archive; p. 16 (5): Getty Images/Sonja Flemming/CBS; p. 16 (6): Getty Images/Alexander Tamargo; p. 16 (7): Alamy/©Pictoria Press Ltd; p. 16 (8): Alamy/©Zuma Press; p. 16 (9): Getty Images/Steve Granitz/WireImage; p. 17 (CR): Shutterstock Images/Vovan; p. 18 (TL): Shutterstock Images/Mayakova; p. 18 (BL): Alamy/©Newscast; p. 19 (B/G): Shutterstock Images/Made-in-China; p. 19 (TL): Summit Entertainment/The Kobal Collection; p. 20 (TR): Alamy/©Archives Du 7e Art/Ashutosh Gowariker Productions 12; p. 20 (CR): REX/Everett Collection; p. 20 (BR): ©DHARMA PRODUCTIONS//THE KOBAL COLLECTION; p. 20 (BL): Shutterstock Images/Loke Yek Mang; p. 20 (TL): Shutterstock Images/Majcot; p. 21 (BR): Shutterstock Images/Kurhan; p. 22-23 (B/G): Getty Images/John Giustina; p. 23 (1): Getty Images/JupiterImages; p. 23 (2): Alamy/©Patti McConville; p. 23 (3): Alamy/©David R.Frazier; p. 23 (4): Alamy/©Alex Segre; p. 23 (5): Alamy/©Patti McConville; p. 23 (6): Alamy/©Lain Masterton; p. 23 (7): Alamy/©P.D.Amedzro; p. 23 (8): Alamy/©Jader Alto; p. 23 (9): Alamy/©Thomas Cockrem; p. 23 (10): Alamy/©Kim Kaminski; p. 23 (11): Shutterstock Images/Racorn; p. 24 (T): Alamy/©Robert Harding Picture Library Ltd; p. 24 (a): Alamy/©Caro; p. 24 (b): Alamy/©D. Hurst; p. 24 (c): Getty Images/Richard I'Anson/Lonely Planet Images; p. 24 (d): Alamy/©Laborant; p. 25 (BR): Corbis/2/Jack Hollingsworth/Ocean; p. 26 (TL): Corbis/Image Source; p. 27 (B): Shutterstock Images/Mark Poprocki; p. 28 (TL): Shutterstock Images/Dmitry Kalinovsky; p. 28 (BL): Shutterstock Images/Elnur; p. 29 (TR): Shutterstock Images/Sashkin; p. 29 (TL): Shutterstock Images/John Kasawa; p. 30 (T): Alamy/©ZUMA Press, Inc; p. 30 (C): Shutterstock Images/Dragi52; p. 30 (TR): Shutterstock Images/Joost Van Uffelen; p. 30 (B/G): Shutterstock Images/Angela Waye; p. 31 (1): Shutterstock Images/Diplomatia; p. 31 (2): Shutterstock Images/Lendy16; p. 31 (3): Alamy/©D. Hurst; p. 31 (4): Shutterstock Images/Studio Smart; p. 31 (5): Shutterstock Images/MTrebbin; p. 31 (6): Shutterstock Images/Julian Rovagnati; p. 32 (C): Corbis/Blue Images; p. 32-33 (B/G): Shutterstock Images/Neirfy; p. 33 (1): Thinkstock/mark wragg/iStock; p. 33 (2): Shutterstock Images/Brocreative; p. 33 (3): Shutterstock Images/Monika Wisniewska; p. 33 (4): Shutterstock Images/yamix; p. 33 (5): Getty Images/Maria Pereira Photography/Flickr; p. 33 (6): Corbis/Beau Lark; p. 33 (7): Alamy/©Shotshop GmbH; p. 33 (8): Shutterstock Images/Dmitry Yashkin; p. 33 (9): Alamy/©IE235/Image Source Plus; p. 33 (10): Shutterstock Images/mezzotint; p. 34 (TL): Getty Images/Stephen Dunn; p. 34 (TC): Getty Images/Matthew Lloyd/Bloomberg; p. 34 (TR): REX/Theo Kingma; p. 35 (TR): Alamy/©Photos 12; p. 36 (T): Shutterstock Images/Nils Petersen; p. 36 (a): Alamy/©Jack Hollingsworth/Blend Images; p. 36 (b): Shutterstock Images/Oliveromg; p. 36 (c): Alamy/©KidStock/Blend Images; p. 36 (d): Alamy/©Leah Warkentin/Design Pics Inc; p. 36 (e): Alamy/©Ron Dahlquist/Pacific Stock; p. 36 (f): Shutterstock Images/Piotr Marcinski; p. 36 (g): Alamy/©Kalle Singer/Beyond Fotomedia GmbH; p. 36 (h): Shutterstock Images/Aleksandr Markin; p. 36 (i): Alamy/©Arco Images/De Meester; p. 37 (TR): Shutterstock Images/Shvak; p. 37 (TCR): Shutterstock Images/Rarach; p. 37 (BCR): Getty Images/Image Source; p. 37 (BR): Shutterstock Images/Murengstockphoto; p. 38 (BL): Alamy/©David Grossman; p. 38 (TL): Alamy/©Rosanne Tackaberry; p. 39 (B/G): Getty Images/Jerritt Clark/Stringer; p. 39 (TL): Alamy/©Zuma Press Inc; p. 40 (TL): Shutterstock Images/Pascal Le Segretain; p. 40 (B): Shutterstock Images/Kjersti Joergensen; p. 40 (C): Getty Images/Cameron Spencer; p. 41 (1): Shutterstock Images/Wavebreakmedia; p. 41 (2): Alamy/©PCN Photography; p. 41 (3): Shutterstock Images/Darren Baker; p. 41 (4): Alamy/©[apply pictures]; p. 42-43 (B/G): Getty Images/Marko Stavric Photography; p. 46 (T): Shutterstock Images/Mindscape Studio; p. 46 (1): Alamy/©Agencja Free; p. 46 (2): Alamy/©Blickwinkel; p. 46 (3): Shutterstock Images/Khwi; p. 46 (4): Getty Images/Danita Delimont; p. 46 (5): Shutterstock Images/Catalin Petolea; p. 46 (6): Shutterstock Images/Jarry; p. 46 (7): Alamy/©Phovoir; p. 46 (8): Shutterstock Images/Golden Pixels LLC; p. 46 (9): Shutterstock Images/Gow27; p. 47 (T): Corbis/Erik Isakson/Blend Images; p. 48 (BL): Alamy/©MasPix; p. 48 (CL): Alamy/©Blickwinkel; p. 50 (TR): REX/Courtesy Everett Collection; p. 50 (CR): Getty Images/Jeff Neumann/CBS; p. 50 (B/G): Shutterstock Images/Richard Peterson; p. 54-55 (B/G): Corbis/Anna Stowe/LOOP IMAGES; p. 52-52 (BL): Corbis/Elli Thor Magnusson; p. 56 (TL): Shutterstock Images/guentermanaus; p. 56 (CL): Alamy/©Hemis; p. 56 (TR): Shutterstock Images/Marina Jay; p. 56 (B/G): Shutterstock Images/KayaMe; p. 57 (CL): Alamy/©blickwinkel; p. 58 (TL): Getty Images/Chip Simons; p. 58 (1): Shutterstock Images/Big Pants Production; p. 58 (2): Alamy/©Incamerastock; p. 58 (3): Corbis/Ken Kaminesky/Take 2 Productions; p. 58 (4): Shutterstock Images/Shell114; p. 58 (5): Shutterstock Images/Kamil Macniak; p. 58 (6): Shutterstock Images/Ramona Heim; p. 58 (7): Shutterstock Images/Maxim Ibragimov; p. 58 (8): Shutterstock Images/Sergemi; p. 58 (9): Shutterstock Images/HomeArt; p. 58 (10): Getty Images/J.R.Ball; p. 58 (11):Shutterstock Images/Andrey Armyagov; p. 58 (12): Shutterstock Images/Africa Studio; p. 59 (CR): Shutterstock Images/Jaroslav74; p. 60 (T): Shutterstock Images/Africa Studio; p. 60 (BL): Shutterstock Images/Gemenacom; p. 61 (TR): Shutterstock Images/Romakoma; p. 62 (T): Shutterstock Images/FCG; p. 62 (T): Alamy/©Radius Images; p. 62 (CL): Shutterstock Images/EggHeadPhoto; p. 62 (CR): Thinkstock/Stockbyte; p. 62 (BL): Alamy/©Randy Duchaine; p. 62 (B): Shutterstock Images/View Apart; p. 64-65 (B/G): Shutterstock Images/Diversepixel; p. 65 (1): Shutterstock Images/Archiwiz; p. 65 (2): Shutterstock Images/Maksym Dykha; p. 65 (3): Shutterstock Images/AG-PHOTO; p. 65 (4): Shutterstock Images/Alexey Boldin; p. 65 (5): Alamy/©keith morris; p. 65 (6): Shutterstock Images/GeorgeMPhotography; p. 65 (7): Shutterstock Images/Joris van den Heuvel; p. 65 (8): Shutterstock Images/Bloom Design; p. 65 (9): Shutterstock Images/Goldyg; p. 66 (CR): Getty Images/SSPL; p. 66 (T): Shutterstock Images/Sergey Nivens; p. 66 (BR): Shutterstock Images/Joris van den Heuvel; p. 68 (TL): Shutterstock Images/CandyBox Images; p. 68 (a): Shutterstock Images/Showcake; p. 68 (b): Shutterstock Images/Modella; p. 68 (c): Shutterstock Images/Pumkinpie; p. 68 (d): Shutterstock Images/Rob Marmion; p. 68 (e): Shutterstock Images/Mark Sykes; p. 68 (f): Shutterstock Images/Valeri Potapova; p. 68 (g): Alamy/©Maxim Images; p. 69 (CR): Alamy/©Ralph Talmont/Aurora Photos; p. 70 (B): Alamy/©Peter Alvey People; p. 70 (TL): Shutterstock Images/Siberia - Video and Photo; p. 71 (TR): Shutterstock Images/Olga Popova; p. 72 (TL): Shutterstock Images/James Steidl; p. 72 (BR): Alamy/©Ian Dagnall Computing; p. 72 (TR): Shutterstock Images/Fad82; p. 72 (BL): Shutterstock Images/Kitch Bain; p. 72 (B/G): Shutterstock Images/Concept Photo; p. 73 (1): Shutterstock Images/Luis Carlos Torres; p. 73 (2): Shutterstock Images/Maksym Dykha; p. 73 (3): Shutterstock Images/BigKnell; p. 73 (4): Shutterstock Images/Volodymyr Krasyuk; p. 74-75 (B/G): Corbis/Werner Dieterich/Westend61; p. 75 (a): Shutterstock Images/Monkey Business Images; p. 75 (b): Alamy/©Driver's License; p. 75 (c): Alamy/©Cultura Creative; p. 75 (d): Shutterstock Images/Nikola Solev; p. 75 (e): Shutterstock Images/razihusin; p. 75 (f): Shutterstock Images/Joe Gough; p. 75 (g): Shutterstock Images/Karen Grigoryan; p. 75 (h): Alamy/©Ben Molyneux People; p. 75 (i): Corbis/Mark Edward Atkinson/Tracey Lee/Blend Images; p. 75 (j): Shutterstock Images/Monkey Business Images; p. 76 (TL): REX/Bruce Adams;p. 76 (TC): Alamy/©Bill Bachman; p. 77 (BL): Shutterstock Images/MTrebbin; p. 77 (TL): Shutterstock Images/GeniusKp; p. 77 (TR): Shutterstock Images/Arman Zhenikeyev; p. 77 (BR): Shutterstock Images/Irin-k; p. 78 (T): Alamy/©VStock; p. 78 (1): Shutterstock Images/Carsten Reisinger; p. 78 (2): Shutterstock Images/Rob Hyrons; p. 78 (3): Shutterstock Images/Molodec; p. 78 (4): Shutterstock Images/jocic; p. 78 (5): Shutterstock Images/Worker; p. 78 (6): Shutterstock Images/R. Gino Santa Maria; p. 78 (7): Shutterstock Images/Nikkytok; p. 78 (8): Shutterstock Images/Donatas1205; p. 79 (BR): Getty images/Muammer Mujdat Uzel; p. 80 (TL): Shutterstock Images/Bloomua; p. 80 (BL): Alamy/©Denise Hager Catchlight Visual Services; p. 81 (TR): Getty Images/Juanmonino; p. 82 (BL): Alamy/©Steve Skjold; p. 82 (CL): Alamy/©Alaska Stock; p. 82 (B/G): Shutterstock Images/Galyna Andrushko; p. 82 (TL): Alamy/©Gail Mooney-Kelly; p. 82 (T): Shutterstock Images/Galyna Andrushko; p. 83 (1): Shutterstock Images/Roman Samokhin; p. 83 (2): Shutterstock Images/Hal_P; p. 83 (3): Shutterstock Images/EZeePics Studio; p. 83 (4): Alamy/©Mike Kemp; p. 84-85 (B/G): Corbis/Corey Rich/Aurora Open; p .85 (1): Getty Images/Tammy Bryngelson; p. 85 (2): Alamy/©Rob Stark; p. 85 (3): Shutterstock Images/Apples Eyes Studio; p. 85 (4): Alamy/©Nik Taylor; p. 85 (5): Shutterstock Images/Robert Crum; p. 85 (6): Alamy/©Imagebroker; p. 85 (7): Getty Images/Jason Weddington; p. 85 (8): Corbis/Burger/phanie/Phanie Sarl; p. 85 (9): Shutterstock Images/Piotr Marcinski; p. 85 (10): Shutterstock Images/Mahathir Mohd Yasin; p. 86 (TR): Alamy/©Trekandshoot; p. 86 (TL): Shutterstock Images/Dan Thornberg; p. 86 (TL): Shutterstock Images/Ilya Andriyanov; p. 86 (CL): Shutterstock Images/Filatov Alexey; p. 86 (T): Shutterstock Images/Endeavor; p. 87 (CR): Getty Images/Ebby May; p. 88 (T): Shutterstock Images/Varuna; p. 88 (A): Alamy/©Image Source Plus; p. 88 (BC): Alamy/©Enigma; p. 89 (BR): REX/Andrew Price; p. 90 (TL): Shutterstock Images/Wonderisland; p. 90 (BL): Shutterstock Images/HomeArt; p. 91 (TR): Shutterstock Images/Stefan Pircher; p. 92 (TL): Shutterstock Images/Dr.Morley Read; p. 92 (TC): Shutterstock Images/Kletr; p. 92 (BR): Shutterstock Images/Decha Thapanya; p. 92 (T): Shutterstock Images/Foxy; p. 92 (B/G): Shutterstock Images/Brodtcast; p. 92 (BL): Alamy/©Robert M. Vera; p. 92 (TR): Getty Images/Murray Cooper/Minden Pictures; p. 93 (1,2,3,4): Shutterstock Images/Goa Novi; p. 93 (5,6,7): Shutterstock Images/Flashon Studio; p. 93 (8,9): Shutterstock Images/Iko; p. 94-95 (B/G): Corbis/Tim Pannell; p. 95 (1): Shutterstock Images/Claudia Paulussen; p. 95 (2): Shutterstock Images/Golden Pixels LLC; p. 95 (3): Getty Images/Jupiter Images; p. 95 (4): Shutterstock Images/Christine Langer-Pueschel; p. 95 (5): Shutterstock Images/BlueSkyImage; p. 95 (6): Alamy/©Radius Images; p. 95 (7): Alamy/©Frederic Cirou/PhotoAlto sas; p. 95 (8): Getty Images/Rob Lewine; p. 96 (TC): Getty Images; p. 96 (TR): Alamy/©Gregory James; p. 97 (CL): Alamy/©South West Images Scotland; p. 98 (TL): Getty Images/Mbbirdy; p. 98 (1): Shutterstock Images/Guillermo Del Olmo; p. 98 (3): Shutterstock Images/Patrick Foto; p. 98 (4): Shutterstock Images/PathDoc; p. 98 (5): Shutterstock Images/Arvydas Kniuksta; p. 98 (6): Shutterstock Images/Sabphoto; p. 98 (7): Shutterstock Images/Sashahaltam; p. 98 (8): Shutterstock Images/Tracy Whiteside; p. 98 (9): Shutterstock Images/Elena Elisseeva; p. 98 (10): Shutterstock Images/Jeka; p. 100 (TL): Getty Images/Nancy R.Cohen; p. 100 (BL): Shutterstock Images/SW Productions/Photodisc; p. 101 (TR): Alamy/©View Pictures Ltd; p. 102 (B): Shutterstock Images/Roman Sigaev; p. 102 (TR): Shutterstock Images/Focuslight; p. 103 (1): Shutterstock Images/Denise Kappa; p. 103 (2): Shutterstock Images/Studio Vin; p. 103 (3): Alamy/©Niehoff/Imagebroker; p. 103 (4): Shutterstock Images/Taelove7; p. 103 (5): Shutterstock Images/Artiis; p. 103 (6): Shutterstock Images/Aerogondo2; p. 104-105 (B/G): Shutterstock Images/Alexander Vershinin; p. 116 (T): Getty Images/Javier Pierini; p. 117 (T): Shutterstock Images/Jktu_21; Back cover: Shutterstock Images/Vibrant Image Studio.

Front cover photography by Alamy/©Marc Hill.

The publishers are grateful to the following illustrators:

David Belmonte p. 44; Nigel Dobbyn p. 43, 49, 102; Q2A Media Services, Inc. p. 7, 55, 63, 118; Jose Rubio p. 26, 119; Sean Tiffany p. 7.

All video stills by kind permission of:

Discovery Communications, LLC 2015: p. 2 (1, 3), 5, 10, 12 (1, 3, 4), 15, 20, 21, 22 (1, 3), 25, ̶ ̶32 (1, ̶ ̶, 4), 35, 40, 41 ̶ ̶ ̶ ̶3, 4), 45, 50, 51, 54 (1, 3), 57, 62, 64 (1, 3, 4), 67, 72, 73, 74 (1, 3), 77, 82, 84 (1, 3), 87, 92, 94 (1, 3, 4), 97, 102, 103, 116, 117, 118, 119, 120; Cambr̶ ̶ ̶ ̶ University Pr̶ess: p. ̶ ̶ ̶ 12 (2), 18, 22 (2), 28, 32 (2), 38, 42 (2), 48, 54 (2), 60, 64 (2), 70, 72 (2), 80, 84 (2), 90, 94 (2), 100.